특목고 · 내신 대비 어휘 정복 프로젝트!!

Top Vocabulary

Worldcom Contents Development Team

중급
Level 1

WorldCom ELT

Preface

수많은 어휘 교재가 출간되었음에도 불구하고 학생들의 단어 실력을 체계적이고 효율적으로 길러주는 책을 찾기가 몹시도 어려운 실정입니다. 시험에서 활용도가 떨어지는 불필요한 사항만을 다루거나 무조건 외우게 하여 학습 부담을 가중시키거나 다양한 영어 시험에 대비해야 하는 우리 학생들의 실정에 걸맞지 않는 교재들이 흔합니다.

Top Vocabulary는 이와 같은 현실을 개선하기 위하여 탄생한 어휘 교재입니다. 학생들이 단어를 익힐 수 있도록 구성된 다양한 문제를 해결하면서 익힐 수 있도록 하였습니다.

영어 공부에 있어서 문법을 바로 알고 독해력을 습득하는 것은 매우 중요합니다. 그러나 이것을 이루기 위해서는 기본적이며 필수적인 단어를 외우는 능력, 즉 어휘력이 그 첫 번째가 됩니다. 영어를 잘하기 위해서는 많이 듣고, 읽고, 말하고, 쓰는 연습을 해야 합니다. 그런데 말이란 여러 개의 단어들로 구성되어 있으니 단어를 잘 알아야 영어 능력이 향상시킬 수
있습니다.

영어 단어를 보다 효율적으로 익히려면 반복하여 읽고 쓰는 연습이 가장 효과적입니다. 하지만 단어를 단순하게 하나 하나 암기하는 것은 곧 잊어버리게 되고, 영어에 대한 흥미도 사라지게 됩니다. 학생 여러분들의 어휘력을 증강시키려면 반드시 실용적인 예문을 많이 읽고, 많이 쓰는 것을 반복하십시오.

부디 중도에서 포기하지 말고 끝까지 노력하시길 바랍니다. 그렇게 하면 여러분이 앞으로 도전할 각종 시험에서 고득점을 성취하실 수 있게 됩니다.
여러분의 건투를 빕니다.

여러분을 단어왕으로 만드는 학습법

반드시 지켜야 할 4계명

1. 연습장이라고 생각하고 빈 공간을 무조건 쓰면서 암기한다
2. 하루라도 거르지 않고 매일 학습한다
3. 적어도 이 책을 3번 반복하여 학습한다
4. 네이티브의 발음을 따라하면서 학습한다

이 책의 4단계 단어 암기법 특징

1단계: **새로운 단어를 3번씩 써보면서 외우기!!**

제시된 단어를 3번씩 써보고, 무료로 제공되는 MP3 화일로 원어민의 정확한 발음을 익히고 따라하자

2단계: **영어는 우리말로, 우리말은 영어로 써보면서 다시 외워보자!!**

영어 실력의 80%는 단어 실력이라는데 우리말을 보면서 영어로 외우고 영어를 우리말로 암기하면 쑥쑥 늘어가는 단어 실력을 느낄 수 있다

3단계: **문장에 알 맞는 단어를 써보면서 외운 단어 확인해보자!!**

암기한 단어를 활용하여 문장에 넣을 수가 있다면 단어에 대한 큰 자신감이 생긴다

4단계: **토플, 토익, 텝스등 각종 시험에 대비하여 영영풀이로 써보면서 자신의 단어 실력을 업그레이드 하자!!**

단어의 뜻을 영영적인 표현으로 익히는 연습을 하면 원서나 각종 영어 시험에도 고득점에 도전할 수 있는 초석을 다지게 된다

TOP Vocabulary 중급 Level 1

Worldcom Contents Development Team

Cover/Interior Design: Joo Design

펴낸이 | 임 병 업
펴낸곳 | (주)월드컴 에듀
등록 | 2000년 1월 17일
주소 | 서울특별시 강남구 도곡동 467-6
대림 아크로텔 C동 1403호
전화 | 02)3273-4300(대표)
팩스 | 02)3273-4303
홈페이지 | www.wcbooks.co.kr
이메일 | wc4300@wcbooks.co.kr

Contents

1일째... 1 ~ 16 6
2일째... 17 ~ 32 10
3일째... 33 ~ 48 14
4일째... 49 ~ 64 18
5일째... 65 ~ 80 22
단어test 1 ~ 5일 26
6일째... 81 ~ 96 28
7일째... 97 ~ 112 32
8일째... 113 ~ 128 36
9일째... 129 ~ 144 40
10일째... 145 ~ 160 44
단어test 6 ~ 10일 48
11일째... 161 ~ 176 50
12일째... 177 ~ 192 54
13일째... 193 ~ 208 58
14일째... 209 ~ 224 62
15일째... 225 ~ 240 66
단어test 11 ~ 15일 70
16일째... 241 ~ 256 72
17일째... 257 ~ 272 76
18일째... 273 ~ 288 80
19일째... 289 ~ 304 84
20일째... 305 ~ 320 88
단어test 16 ~ 20일 92
21일째... 321 ~ 336 94
22일째... 337 ~ 352 98
23일째... 353 ~ 368 102
24일째... 369 ~ 384 106
25일째... 385 ~ 400 110
단어test 21 ~ 25일 114
26일째... 401 ~ 416 116
27일째... 417 ~ 432 120
28일째... 433 ~ 448 124
29일째... 449 ~ 464 128
30일째... 465 ~ 480 132
단어test 26 ~ 30일 136

단어퀴즈 · 정답(별책)

단어공부 1일째

따라하기 | 단어를 세 번씩 따라 써보세요.

1	**approach** [əpróutʃ]	v. 접근하다 n. 통로, 입구		
2	**harm** [hɑːrm]	v. 해치다 n. 해 ▶ harmful : a. 해로운(↔ harmless)		
3	**damage** [dǽmidʒ]	v. 손상시키다 n. 손상, 손해		
4	**attack** [ətǽk]	v. 공격하다(↔defend) n. 공격		
5	**choke** [tʃouk]	v. ❶ 질식시키다 ❷ 질식하다		
6	**bite** [bait]	v. 물다, 물어 뜯다 n. 물기		
7	**blow** [blou]	v. (바람이)불다, (입김으로)불다		
8	**fling** [fliŋ]	v. 내던지다		

연습문제 1 | 영어는 우리말로, 우리말은 영어로 써 보세요.

1. harm ______
2. attack ______
3. bite ______
4. fling ______
5. blow ______
6. choke ______
7. damage ______
8. approach ______

1. 불다 ______
2. 공격하다 ______
3. 접근하다 ______
4. 해치다 ______
5. 내던지다 ______
6. 손상시키다 ______
7. 질식시키다 ______
8. 물어 뜯다 ______

연습문제 2 | 문장에 알맞는 단어를 써 보세요.

1. 비가 열린 창문을 통해 들어와 창턱에 있던 책들을 못쓰게 만들었다.
   Rain came through the open window and ____________ the books on the window sill.

2. 비행기는 공항에 접근했다.
   The plane ____________ the airport.

3. 때로 그는 책들과 코트를 자기 침대에 내던진다.
   Sometimes he just ____________ his books and coat on his bed.

4. 그 개는 사나워 보이지만 당신을 해치지 않을 겁니다.
   The dog looks fierce, but it will not ____________ you.

5. 1950년 6월 25일 북한은 남한을 공격하기 시작했다.
   On June 25, 1950, North Korea began to ____________ South Korea.

6. 온종일 강풍이 불었다.
   The wind ____________ hard all day.

7. 화재에서 나오는 연기로 우리는 숨이 막혔다.
   The smoke from the fire ____________ us.

8. 그 개는 우편배달부의 다리를 물었다.
   The dog ____________ the mail carrier's leg.

연습문제 3 | 영영풀이에 맞는 단어를 써 보세요.

1. ____________ : to hurt, to injure
2. ____________ : to come near to
3. ____________ : to make somebody unable to breathe
4. ____________ : to throw, to toss with force
5. ____________ : to cut with the teeth
6. ____________ : to move with force, as in air
7. ____________ : to fight against
8. ____________ : to injure, to damage

단어공부 1일째

따라하기 단어를 세 번씩 따라 써보세요.

9 **pretend** [priténd]	v. ~인 체하다(= make believe); 가장하다
10 **imitate** [ímitèit]	v. 모방하다 ▶ imitation : n. 모방
11 **affect** [əfékt]	v. 영향을 미치다(= have an effect on)
12 **consider** [kənsídər]	v. 고려하다, 생각하다
13 **pause** [pɔːz]	v. 잠시 중지하다 n. (일시적)중단
14 **amuse** [əmjúːz]	v. 흥겹게 하다, 기쁘게 하다 ▶ amusement : n. 즐거움
15 **dine** [dain]	v. 식사하다
16 **entertain** [èntərtéin]	v. (여흥 따위로)즐겁게 해주다, 위안하다 ▶ entertainment : n. 오락, 여흥

연습문제 1 영어는 우리말로, 우리말은 영어로 써 보세요.

1. imitate ____________
2. pause ____________
3. dine ____________
4. entertain ____________
5. pretend ____________
6. amuse ____________
7. affect ____________
8. consider ____________

1. 영향을 미치다 ____________
2. 식사하다 ____________
3. 모방하다 ____________
4. 즐겁게 해주다 ____________
5. 고려하다 ____________
6. 흥겹게 하다 ____________
7. ~인 체하다 ____________
8. 잠시 중지하다 ____________

연습문제 2 문장에 알맞는 단어를 써 보세요.

1. 나는 캐나다 여행을 생각중이다.
I am ____________ taking a trip to Canada.

2. 그 어릿광대들은 아이들을 즐겁게 했다.
The silly clowns ____________ the children.

3. 사람들은 자기들이 숭배하는 사람들을 종종 모방한다.
People often ____________ other people whom they admire.

4. 나의 부모님들은 결혼기념일에 음식점에서 식사를 하셨다.
My parents ____________ at a restaurant on their anniversary.

5. 아이들은 잠이 든 체했다.
The children ____________ to be asleep.

6. 서커스는 아이들을 즐겁게 해주었다.
The circus ____________ the children.

7. 어른들은 아이들이 따라오게 잠시 멈추었다.
The grown-ups ____________ to let the children catch up.

8. 가뭄은 농작물에 영향을 줄 수 있다.
The lack of rain may ____________ the crops.

연습문제 3 영영풀이에 맞는 단어를 써 보세요.

1. ____________ : to think about carefully
2. ____________ : to eat dinner
3. ____________ : to act the same way as someone
4. ____________ : to make people interested
5. ____________ : to make believe
6. ____________ : to stop for a short time
7. ____________ : to make someone laugh
8. ____________ : to cause some change

단어공부 2일째

따라하기 단어를 세 번씩 따라 써보세요.

17 **excite** [iksáit]	v. 흥분시키다, 자극하다 ▶ excited / exciting : a. 흥분한 / 흥분시키는
18 **thrill** [θril]	v. 가슴 설레게 하다 n. 가슴 설렘
19 **amaze** [əméiz]	v. 몹시 놀라게 하다 ▶ amazing : a. 놀라운 / amazement : n. 경탄
20 **smash** [smæʃ]	v. 박살내다 n. 박살냄
21 **astonish** [əstɑ́niʃ]	v. 깜짝 놀라게 하다(= amaze)
22 **impress** [imprés]	v. 깊은 인상을 주다, 감동시키다 ▶ impressive : a. 인상적인, 감명을 주는
23 **reap** [ri:p]	v. (곡물을) 수확하다, 거둬들이다
24 **faint** [feint]	v. 졸도하다(= pass out) a. 희미한, 어렴풋한

연습문제 1 영어는 우리말로, 우리말은 영어로 써 보세요.

1. amaze ______
2. smash ______
3. astonish ______
4. faint ______
5. reap ______
6. excite ______
7. impress ______
8. thrill ______

1. 졸도하다 ______
2. 깜짝 놀라게 하다 ______
3. 박살내다 ______
4. 몹시 놀라게 하다 ______
5. 흥분시키다 ______
6. 수확하다 ______
7. 가슴 설레게 하다 ______
8. 깊은 인상을 주다 ______

연습문제 2 문장에 알맞는 단어를 써 보세요.

1. 그녀는 그를 만났을 때 정말 가슴이 설레었다.
   She was really ____________ to meet him.

2. 경연대회에서 내가 입상했다는 소식에 나는 깜짝 놀랐다.
   The news that I had won the contest ____________ me.

3. 밴쿠버의 경관은 언제나 외국 관광객들에게 깊은 인상을 준다.
   The sights of Vancouver never fail to ____________ foreign tourists.

4. 두 명의 관중이 경기장의 더위로 인해 졸도했다.
   Two spectators ____________ from the heat in the stadium.

5. 농장의 일꾼들이 밀을 수확하고 있다.
   The farm hands are ____________ their wheat.

6. 그 아이가 수학문제를 푸는 속도에 우리는 매우 놀랐다.
   The child's speed at solving mathematical problems ____________ us.

7. 그는 논쟁 중에 매우 흥분했다.
   He got very ____________ during the argument.

8. 접시가 떨어져 마루에 박살났다.
   The plate fell and ____________ on the floor.

연습문제 3 영영풀이에 맞는 단어를 써 보세요.

1. ____________ : to surprise greatly
2. ____________ : to make someone have strong feelings of
3. ____________ : to pass out
4. ____________ : to surprise greatly
5. ____________ : to make someone feel excited
6. ____________ : to cut down and collect
7. ____________ : to break something
8. ____________ : to produce a strong effect on the mind

단어공부 2일째

따라하기 단어를 세 번씩 따라 써보세요.

25 **fold** [fould]	v. 접다; (손·팔을) 끼다
26 **drift** [drift]	v. (바람·물결에) 표류하다, 떠내려가다
27 **recite** [risáit]	v. 암송하다, 낭송하다 ▶ recitation : n. 암송, 낭송
28 **imagine** [imǽdʒin]	v. 상상하다, 생각하다 ▶ imaginative : a. 상상력이 풍부한
29 **assume** [əsúːm]	v. 가정하다 ▶ assumption : n. 가정
30 **split** [split]	v. ❶ 쪼개다 ❷ 나누다
31 **commit** [kəmít]	v. 저지르다
32 **doubt** [daut]	v. 의심하다

연습문제 1 영어는 우리말로, 우리말은 영어로 써 보세요.

1. recite ____________
2. split ____________
3. drift ____________
4. commit ____________
5. doubt ____________
6. fold ____________
7. imagine ____________
8. assume ____________

1. 표류하다 ____________
2. 상상하다 ____________
3. 의심하다 ____________
4. 쪼개다 ____________
5. 저지르다 ____________
6. 가정하다 ____________
7. 접다 ____________
8. 암송하다 ____________

연습문제 2 문장에 알맞는 단어를 써 보세요.

1. 입에서 불을 토하는 용을 상상해 봐.
______________ a dragon breathing fire.

2. 보트는 물가로 표류했다.
The boat ______________ toward the shore.

3. 판사는 죄수가 진실을 말하고 있다는 것을 의심했다.
The judge ______________ that the prisoner was telling the truth.

4. 이 통나무들을 땔감용으로 쪼개세요.
______________ these logs for firewood.

5. 나는 편지를 접어 봉투에 넣었다.
I ______________ the letter and put it in the envelope.

6. 그는 살인을 했기 때문에 처벌돼야 한다.
He has ______________ murder and must be punished.

7. 그는 그들에게 성경을 낭송했다.
He ______________ the Bible to them.

8. 내일 비가 온다고 가정하면 우린 뭘 하지?
______________ it rains tomorrow, what shall we do?

연습문제 3 영영풀이에 맞는 단어를 써 보세요.

1. ______________ : to repeat a piece of writing from memory

2. ______________ : to do something bad

3. ______________ : to think to be true

4. ______________ : to be moved by water or wind

5. ______________ : to be not sure of

6. ______________ : to make a picture in the mind

7. ______________ : to divide into different parts

8. ______________ : to bend something so that one part covers another

단어공부 3일째

따라하기 단어를 세 번씩 따라 써보세요.

33	**suspect** [səspékt]	v. ~라고 생각하다, 의심하다(= doubt) ▶ suspicious : a. 의심하는
34	**shrug** [ʃrʌg]	v. (어깨를) 움츠리다 n. 어깨를 으쓱함(의심·무관심을 나타내는 몸 동작)
35	**collide** [kəláid]	v. 충돌하다 ▶ collision : n. 충돌
36	**intend** [inténd]	v. 의도하다, ~할 작정이다 ▶ intention : n. 의도
37	**decide** [disáid]	v. 결정하다, 결심하다 ▶ decision : n. 결정, 결심
38	**accomplish** [əkámpliʃ]	v. 이룩하다, 완수하다 ▶ accomplished : a. (기예에) 통달한
39	**shrink** [ʃriŋk]	v. 줄다 ▶ shrinkage : n. 수축
40	**gain** [gein]	v. 얻다(= get)

연습문제 1 영어는 우리말로, 우리말은 영어로 써 보세요.

1. collide ____________
2. accomplish ____________
3. gain ____________
4. intend ____________
5. suspect ____________
6. decide ____________
7. shrink ____________
8. shrug ____________

1. 의도하다 ____________
2. ~라고 생각하다 ____________
3. 줄다 ____________
4. 충돌하다 ____________
5. 움츠리다 ____________
6. 이룩하다 ____________
7. 얻다 ____________
8. 결심하다 ____________

연습문제 2 문장에 알맞는 단어를 써 보세요.

1. 우리는 너무 늦어 거기에 안 가기로 했다.
   We ____________ that it was too late to go there.

2. 그 차와 버스가 모퉁이에서 충돌했다.
   The car and the bus ____________ at the corner.

3. 나는 그들이 이미 떠났다고 생각한다.
   I ____________ that they have already gone.

4. 우리는 계획했던 것보다 더 많은 일을 이룩했다.
   We ____________ more work than we had planned.

5. 나는 그에게 편지를 쓸 작정이었었는데(그만 그렇게 하지 못했다).
   I ____________ to have written to him.

6. 너는 그 상점에서 일하면 경험을 얻을 것이다.
   You will ____________ experience by working at the store.

7. 나는 그녀에게 톰이 어디 있냐고 물었는데 그녀는 그저 어깨를 움츠렸다.
   I asked her where Tom was but she just ____________.

8. 모직 스웨터를 더운 물에 빨면 줄어든다.
   If you wash the wool sweater in hot water, it will ____________.

연습문제 3 영영풀이에 맞는 단어를 써 보세요.

1. ____________ : to hit against
2. ____________ : to succeed in doing something
3. ____________ : to think that something is probably true
4. ____________ : to become smaller, shorter or less
5. ____________ : to plan to do
6. ____________ : to win
7. ____________ : to move one’s shoulders to show doubt, etc.
8. ____________ : to think carefully and choose

단어공부 3일째

따라하기 단어를 세 번씩 따라 써보세요.

41 **emit** [imít]	v. (빛·열·소리·가스를) 내뿜다, 발하다 ▶ emission : n. 방사, 발산
42 **locate** [lóukeit]	v. (장소를) 찾아내다, (장소를) 정하다
43 **long** [lɔːŋ]	v. 갈망하다
44 **achieve** [ətʃíːv]	v. 달성하다, 획득하다 ▶ achievement : n. 달성; 업적; 학력
45 **determine** [ditə́ːrmin]	v. 결정하다 ▶ determination : n. 결심
46 **perform** [pərfɔ́ːrm]	v. ❶ 수행하다 (= carry out) ❷ 공연하다
47 **gather** [gǽðər]	v. ❶ 모으다 (= collect) ❷ 모이다
48 **cling** [kliŋ]	v. 달라붙다 (= stick to), 고수하다

연습문제 1 영어는 우리말로, 우리말은 영어로 써 보세요.

1. determine ________	1. 내뿜다 ________
2. locate ________	2. 갈망하다 ________
3. gather ________	3. 수행하다 ________
4. long ________	4. (장소를) 찾아내다 ________
5. achieve ________	5. 달성하다 ________
6. perform ________	6. 달라붙다 ________
7. emit ________	7. 모으다 ________
8. cling ________	8. 결정하다 ________

연습문제 2 문장에 알맞는 단어를 써 보세요.

1. 너는 좀더 열심히 일하지 않으면 아무것도 달성하지 못할 것이다.
   You will never ____________ anything unless you work harder.

2. 그 의사는 어려운 수술을 했다.
   The doctor ____________ a difficult operation.

3. 어린이들은 때때로 무서울 때 부모곁에 달라붙는다.
   Small children sometimes ____________ to their parents when they are frightened.

4. 나는 내 책들을 탁자에서 모아 치웠다.
   I ____________ my books from the table and put them away.

5. 클럽 회원들은 다음 번 회의 일자를 결정했다.
   The club members ____________ the date for their next meeting.

6. 나는 나의 옛 친구들을 다시 만나기를 갈망했다.
   I ____________ to see my old friends again.

7. 태양은 빛과 열을 내뿜는다.
   The sun ____________ light and heat.

8. 그는 잃어버린 책을 찾을 수 없었다.
   He could not ____________ his lost book.

연습문제 3 영영풀이에 맞는 단어를 써 보세요.

1. ____________ : to want very much
2. ____________ : to come together in a place
3. ____________ : to decide or arrange
4. ____________ : to give off
5. ____________ : to hold closely
6. ____________ : to find out where something is
7. ____________ : to do or carry out
8. ____________ : to get or attain by effort

단어공부 4일째

따라하기 단어를 세 번씩 따라 써보세요.

49 **skip** [skip]	v. 건너뛰다, 넘어가다
50 **connect** [kənékt]	v. 연결하다
51 **vote** [vout]	v. 투표하다　n. 투표
52 **quarrel** [kwɔ́ːrəl]	v. 다투다　n. 말다툼
53 **misunderstand** [mìsʌndərstǽnd]	v. 오해하다　▶ misunderstanding : n. 오해
54 **judge** [dʒʌdʒ]	v. 판단하다　n. 재판관, 판사
55 **educate** [édʒukèit]	v. 교육하다　▶ education : n. 교육
56 **acquire** [əkwáiər]	v. 습득하다　▶ acquired : a. 후천적인

연습문제 1 영어는 우리말로, 우리말은 영어로 써 보세요.

1. vote ________
2. misunderstand ________
3. quarrel ________
4. skip ________
5. educate ________
6. acquire ________
7. judge ________
8. connect ________

1. 투표하다 ________
2. 연결하다 ________
3. 오해하다 ________
4. 판단하다 ________
5. 습득하다 ________
6. 교육하다 ________
7. 다투다 ________
8. 건너뛰다 ________

연습문제 2 문장에 알맞는 단어를 써 보세요.

1. 그 부부는 끊임없이 다투더니 드디어 이혼했다.
The couple ____________ constantly and finally got a divorce.

2. 20세 이상의 사람들만 선거에서 투표할 수 있다.
Only people over 20 can ____________ in the election.

3. 나는 그 지시사항을 오해하여 답을 잉크가 아니고 연필로 썼다.
I ____________ the instructions and wrote my answers in pencil instead of ink.

4. 끊지말고 기다리세요. 연결해 드릴 테니까요.
Please hold the line. I'm trying to ____________ you.

5. 학생들의 대학 교육비는 매우 높다.
The cost of ____________ students at college is very high.

6. 나는 뉴욕에 사는 동안 영어회화 능력을 습득했다.
I ____________ the ability to speak English while I lived in New York.

7. 그 연사는 한 주제에서 다음 주제로 건너뛰어 모두를 어리둥절하게 했다.
The speaker ____________ from one topic to the next, confusing everyone.

8. 그 사고에 누가 책임이 있는지는 판단하기 어려웠다.
It was difficult to ____________ who was responsible for the accident.

연습문제 3 영영풀이에 맞는 단어를 써 보세요.

1. ____________ : to change subjects
2. ____________ : to understand wrongly
3. ____________ : to get something by effort
4. ____________ : to give an opinion about
5. ____________ : to choose a candidate in an election
6. ____________ : to teach someone
7. ____________ : to argue very angrily
8. ____________ : to join one thing to another

단어공부 4일째

따라하기 단어를 세 번씩 따라 써보세요.

57 **ban** [bæn]	v. 금지하다 n. 금지
58 **obtain** [əbtéin]	v. (노력으로) 획득하다 (= come by)
59 **stick** [stik]	v. 들러붙다, 고수하다
60 **rub** [rʌb]	v. 문지르다, 비비다
61 **blush** [blʌʃ]	v. (얼굴을) 붉히다, (얼굴이) 붉어지다
62 **grind** [graind]	v. 갈다
63 **chop** [tʃɑp]	v. 쳐서[찍어] 자르다, 잘게 썰다
64 **communicate** [kəmjúːnikèit]	v. 연락하다

연습문제 1 영어는 우리말로, 우리말은 영어로 써 보세요.

1. grind ______
2. ban ______
3. communicate ______
4. obtain ______
5. chop ______
6. rub ______
7. blush ______
8. stick ______

1. 들러붙다 ______
2. 금지하다 ______
3. 문지르다 ______
4. 붉히다 ______
5. 갈다 ______
6. 연락하다 ______
7. 쳐서 자르다 ______
8. 획득하다 ______

연습문제 2 문장에 알맞는 단어를 써 보세요.

1. 그녀는 햇빛에 탄 팔에 로션을 발라 문질렀다.
   She ____________ lotion on her sunburned arms.

2. 우리는 정육점 주인이 고기를 가는 것을 지켜 보았다.
   We watched the butcher ____________ the meat.

3. 소방대원은 도끼로 문을 찍어내려야 했다.
   The firefighter had to ____________ the door down with an ax.

4. 소금은 바닷물에서 얻을 수 있다.
   Salt can be ____________ from sea water.

5. 캠프에 있었을 때 나는 가족과 편지로 연락을 했다.
   When I was at camp, I ____________ with my family by writing letters.

6. 그 수줍은 학생은 선생님의 칭찬을 듣자 얼굴을 붉혔다.
   The shy student ____________ when praised by the teacher.

7. 그는 일을 끝낼 때까지 그 일에 들러붙는다.
   He ____________ to a task until he finishes it.

8. 정부는 국립공원에서의 사냥을 금지했다.
   The government ____________ the hunting of animals in the national park.

연습문제 3 영영풀이에 맞는 단어를 써 보세요.

1. ____________ : to get something through effort
2. ____________ : to crush into small pieces
3. ____________ : to not permit
4. ____________ : to become red from shame, shyness, etc.
5. ____________ : to cut with hard, sharp blows
6. ____________ : to move something back and forth over something else
7. ____________ : to give messages by talking, writing, etc.
8. ____________ : to keep doing something

단어공부 5일째

따라하기 단어를 세 번씩 따라 써보세요.

65	**sting** [stiŋ]	v. 찌르다, 쏘다
66	**stab** [stæb]	v. (단검으로) 찌르다
67	**wring** [riŋ]	v. 비틀어 짜다
68	**pat** [pæt]	v. 가볍게 두드리다
69	**squeeze** [skwiːz]	v. 짜내다
70	**flip** [flip]	v. (손끝으로) 튀기다, 가볍게 털다
71	**set** [set]	v. 정하다, 지정하다
72	**suit** [suːt]	v. 적합하다, 어울리다

연습문제 1 영어는 우리말로, 우리말은 영어로 써 보세요.

1. stab ______
2. pat ______
3. set ______
4. sting ______
5. flip ______
6. suit ______
7. squeeze ______
8. wring ______

1. 비틀어 짜다 ______
2. 짜내다 ______
3. 찌르다 ______
4. 적합하다 ______
5. 정하다 ______
6. (손끝으로)튀기다 ______
7. 가볍게 두드리다 ______
8. (단검으로)찌르다 ______

연습문제 2 문장에 알맞는 단어를 써 보세요.

1. 그는 칼로 그 남자를 찔렀다.
   He ____________ the man with a knife.

2. 그녀는 격려로서 그의 등을 두드려 주었다.
   She ____________ him on the back in encouragement.

3. 그는 오렌지에서 주스를 짜냈다.
   He ____________ the juice from an orange.

4. 우리는 누가 먼저 갈 것인지 동전을 튀기기로 했다.
   We decided to ____________ a coin to see who would go first.

5. 벌은 쏘는 곤충의 한 종류이다.
   A bee is one kind of insect that ____________.

6. 초록색 재킷이 너에게 아주 잘 어울린다.
   The green jacket ____________ you perfectly.

7. 수건의 물을 짜서 걸으세요.
   ____________ the water out of the towel and hang it up.

8. 그들은 파티날짜를 정했습니까?
   Have they ____________ a date for the party?

연습문제 3 영영풀이에 맞는 단어를 써 보세요.

1. ____________ : to push a knife, etc. into somebody
2. ____________ : to press something hard to get liquid out of it
3. ____________ : to fix (a time, date, etc.)
4. ____________ : to prick or hurt someone
5. ____________ : to tap with a soft, light touch
6. ____________ : to look well on
7. ____________ : to toss or move with the fingers
8. ____________ : to twist or squeeze with force

단어공부 5일째

따라하기 단어를 세 번씩 따라 써보세요.

73 **tame** [teim]	v. 길들이다 a. 길들인
74 **stack** [stæk]	v. 쌓아올리다(= pile) n. 더미, 서가
75 **tie** [tai]	v. ❶ 매다 ❷ 동점이 되다
76 **tack** [tæk]	v. (압정으로) 고정시키다
77 **crawl** [krɔːl]	v. 기다, 기어가다
78 **drown** [draun]	v. 익사하다
79 **save** [seiv]	v. ❶ 구조하다 ❷ 면하게 하다
80 **wake** [weik]	v. ❶ 깨우다 ❷ 깨다

연습문제 1 영어는 우리말로, 우리말은 영어로 써 보세요.

1. tie ______	1. 고정시키다 ______
2. tame ______	2. 깨우다 ______
3. tack ______	3. 익사하다 ______
4. wake ______	4. 구조하다 ______
5. crawl ______	5. 길들이다 ______
6. save ______	6. 쌓아올리다 ______
7. drown ______	7. 기다 ______
8. stack ______	8. 매다 ______

연습문제 2 | 문장에 알맞는 단어를 써 보세요.

1. 방 벽들에 압정으로 포스터를 붙이자.
Let's _____________ posters to the walls of the room.

2. 그 수영 선수는 너무 멀리 나가 익사할 뻔 했다.
The swimmer went out too far and almost _____________.

3. 책들을 구석에 쌓으세요.
Please _____________ the books in the corner.

4. 조용히 하지 않으면 아기가 깰 거야.
Be quiet or you will _____________ the baby.

5. 소방대원들은 타오르는 건물에서 그 여자를 구조했다.
The firefighters _____________ the woman from the burning building.

6. 그의 손이 등 뒤로 묶여 있었다.
His hands were _____________ behind his back.

7. 저 목장에서는 야생마들을 길들인다.
They _____________ wild horses at that ranch.

8. 지렁이들은 땅에서 몸뚱이를 끌면서 기어 간다.
Worms _____________ by pulling their bodies along the ground.

연습문제 3 | 영영풀이에 맞는 단어를 써 보세요.

1. _____________ : to fasten something with tacks

2. _____________ : to pile up

3. _____________ : to die underwater

4. _____________ : to bind something with a string, etc.

5. _____________ : to stop sleeping

6. _____________ : to walk low and carefully

7. _____________ : to make animals less wild

8. _____________ : to keep someone out of harm, etc.

단어 test 1~5일

A 알맞은 단어를 골라서 쓰시오.

shrugged	performed	longed	recited	amused

1. The silly clowns ____________ the children.
2. He ____________ the Bible to them.
3. I asked her where Tom was but she just ____________ .
4. The doctor ____________ a difficult operation.
5. I ____________ to see my old friends again.

B 빈칸에 들어갈 알맞은 단어를 고르시오.

1. He could not ____________ his lost book.
   a. place b. set c. locate d. settle
2. When I was at camp, I ____________ with my family by writing letters.
   a. communicated b. declared c. proclaimed d. conveyed
3. The firefighters ____________ the woman from the burning building.
   a. came b. put c. established d. saved
4. Worms ____________ by pulling their bodies along the ground.
   a. walk b. crawl c. play d. enjoy
5. The wind ____________ hard all day.
   a. exploded b. contacted c. blew d. made

C 빈칸에 들어갈 단어의 알맞은 형태를 고르시오.

1. People often ____________ other people whom they admire.
   a. imitation b. imitate c. imitative

2. The children ____________ to be asleep.
   a. pretended b. pretense c. pretension

3. The news that I had won the contest ____________ me.
   a. astonishing b. astonishment c. astonished

4. We ____________ that it was too late to go there.
   a. decided b. decision c. decisive

5. The club members ____________ the date for their next meeting.
   a. determination b. determinant c. determined

D 다음 주어진 동사를 문맥에 맞게 고치시오.

1. You will (gain)____________ experience by working at the store.

2. I (acquire)____________ the ability to speak English while I lived in New York.

3. Salt can be (obtain)____________ from sea water.

4. The cost of (educate)____________ students at college is very high.

5. He has (commit)____________ murder and must be punished.

단어공부 6일째

따라하기 단어를 세 번씩 따라 써보세요.

81 **boil** [bɔil]	v. ❶ 끓이다, 삶다 ❷ 끓다
82 **leak** [liːk]	v. ❶ 새다 ❷ 새게 하다; 누설하다
83 **bathe** [beið]	v. ❶ 목욕하다(= take a bath) ❷ 씻다(= wash)
84 **mix** [miks]	v. ❶ 섞다(= blend) ❷ 섞이다, 어울리다
85 **lure** [luər]	v. 끌다, 유인하다(= attract) n. 매력, 유인물
86 **roast** [roust]	v. 굽다, 볶다
87 **stare** [stɛər]	v. 빤히 쳐다보다, 응시하다(= gaze)
88 **glance** [glæns]	v. 흘끗 보다 n. 흘끗 봄

연습문제 1 영어는 우리말로, 우리말은 영어로 써 보세요.

1. bathe ______	1. 섞다 ______
2. boil ______	2. 목욕하다 ______
3. lure ______	3. 굽다 ______
4. roast ______	4. 빤히 쳐다보다 ______
5. glance ______	5. 끓이다 ______
6. leak ______	6. 흘끗 보다 ______
7. stare ______	7. 끌다 ______
8. mix ______	8. 새다 ______

연습문제 2 문장에 알맞는 단어를 써 보세요.

1. 나는 취침 전에 늘 목욕을 한다.
   I always ____________ before going to bed.

2. 우리는 음악소리에 끌려 공원으로 갔다.
   We were ____________ to the park by the sound of music.

3. 우리는 저녁식사로 닭을 구웠다.
   We ____________ a chicken for dinner.

4. 화학물질을 섞을 때는 폭발하지 않게 주의하세요.
   When you ____________ the chemicals, be careful that they do not explode.

5. 그녀는 비가 그쳤는지 보려고 창밖을 흘끗 보았다.
   She ____________ out of the window to see if the rain had stopped.

6. 커피 물을 좀 끓이자.
   Let's ____________ some water for coffee.

7. 작은 소년은 상점에 있는 그 이상한 남자를 빤히 쳐다보았다.
   The little boy ____________ at the strange man at the store.

8. 빗물이 지붕의 틈새로 새고 있다.
   The rain is ____________ in through a crack in the roof.

연습문제 3 영영풀이에 맞는 단어를 써 보세요.

1. ____________ : to look at someone or something steadily
2. ____________ : to escape through a small opening or hole
3. ____________ : to trick into doing something
4. ____________ : to quickly look at something
5. ____________ : to wash
6. ____________ : to heat a liquid until it becomes very hot
7. ____________ : to put different things together to make something
8. ____________ : to cook at a high temperature, as in an oven

단어공부 6일째

따라하기 단어를 세 번씩 따라 써보세요.

89 **scan** [skæn]	v. ❶ 훑어보다 ❷ 자세히 보다
90 **cover** [kʌ́vər]	v. ❶ 덮다, 가리다 ❷ 포함하다, 다루다(= deal with)
91 **preserve** [prizə́ːrv]	v. 보존하다, 보호하다 ▶ preservation : n. 보존, 보호
92 **reserve** [rizə́ːrv]	v. 예약하다 ▶ reservation : n. 예약
93 **serve** [səːrv]	v. 제공하다
94 **digest** [daidʒést]	v. 소화하다 ▶ digestion : n. 소화
95 **consume** [kənsúːm]	v. 소비하다(↔produce) ▶ consumer : n. 소비자
96 **appreciate** [əpríːʃièit]	v. ❶ 감사하다 ❷ 감상하다 ❸ (진가를) 인정하다

연습문제 1 영어는 우리말로, 우리말은 영어로 써 보세요.

1. cover ________	1. 보존하다 ________
2. reserve ________	2. 제공하다 ________
3. digest ________	3. 감사하다 ________
4. scan ________	4. 소비하다 ________
5. appreciate ________	5. 소화하다 ________
6. consume ________	6. 훑어보다 ________
7. serve ________	7. 덮다 ________
8. preserve ________	8. 예약하다 ________

연습문제 2 문장에 알맞는 단어를 써 보세요.

1. 우리는 우리의 천연자원을 보존해야 한다.
We must _____________ our natural resources.

2. 극장에 전화해서 좌석 셋을 예약하세요.
Call the theater and _____________ three seats.

3. 그녀는 파란색 식탁보로 테이블 위를 덮었다.
She _____________ the table with a blue tablecloth.

4. 음식이 제대로 소화될 수 있도록 잘 씹으세요.
Chew your food well so it can be _____________ properly.

5. 당신이 이런 볼 일을 대신 해줘 고맙다.
I _____________ your running these errands for me.

6. 큰 차들은 연료를 많이 소비한다.
Big cars _____________ a lot of fuel.

7. 나는 보통 신문의 표제들만 훑어본다.
I only _____________ the newspaper headlines.

8. 조식은 오전 8시에서 10시 사이에 제공된다.
Breakfast is _____________ between 8 and 10 a.m.

연습문제 3 영영풀이에 맞는 단어를 써 보세요.

1. _____________ : to change food into a state in which the body can absorb it
2. _____________ : to place something over
3. _____________ : to be thankful for something
4. _____________ : to glance at something quickly
5. _____________ : to save a place in a hotel, etc.
6. _____________ : to use something up
7. _____________ : to keep in the same condition
8. _____________ : to bring food, etc. to someone

단어공부 7일째

따라하기 단어를 세 번씩 따라 써보세요.

97	**congratulate** [kəngrǽtʃəlèit]	v. 축하하다 ▶ congratulation : n. 축하
98	**compete** [kəmpí:t]	v. 경쟁하다 ▶ competition : n. 경쟁
99	**attend** [əténd]	v. 출석[참석]하다 ▶ attendance : n. 출석[참석]; 참석자 수
100	**navigate** [nǽvigeit]	v. 항해[비행]하다 ▶ navigation : n. 항해[비행]
101	**thrive** [θraiv]	v. 번성[번창]하다
102	**fasten** [fǽsn]	v. 단단히 매다
103	**export** [ékspɔ:rt] [ikspɔ́:rt]	v. 수출하다 n. 수출(품)[ékspɔ:rt]
104	**import** [ímpɔ:rt] [impɔ́:rt]	v. 수입하다 n. 수입(품)[ímpɔ:rt]

연습문제 1 영어는 우리말로, 우리말은 영어로 써 보세요.

1. attend ________	1. 축하하다 ________
2. compete ________	2. 항해하다 ________
3. congratulate ________	3. 번성하다 ________
4. import ________	4. 단단히 매다 ________
5. export ________	5. 수입하다 ________
6. thrive ________	6. 수출하다 ________
7. fasten ________	7. 경쟁하다 ________
8. navigate ________	8. 출석하다 ________

연습문제 2 문장에 알맞는 단어를 써 보세요.

1. 나는 오늘 오후 클럽모임에 참석해야 한다.
   I have to ____________ a club meeting this afternoon.
2. 초기 탐험가들은 별자리를 보고 항해하곤 했다.
   Early explorers used to ____________ by the stars.
3. 그 우승컵을 놓고 10개 팀이 경쟁을 벌이고 있다.
   Ten teams are ____________ for the Cup.
4. 브라질은 많은 나라에 커피를 수출한다.
   Brazil ____________ coffee to a lot of countries.
5. 어떤 식물들은 모래 땅에서 번성한다.
   Some plants ____________ in sandy soil.
6. 친구들이 그의 결혼을 축하했다.
   Friends ____________ him on his marriage.
7. 한국은 석유를 전량 수입한다.
   Korea ____________ all of its oil.
8. 안전벨트를 단단히 매세요.
   ____________ your seat belts.

연습문제 3 영영풀이에 맞는 단어를 써 보세요.

1. ____________ : to fix something firmly
2. ____________ : to travel by ship or plane
3. ____________ : to try to win a race, etc.
4. ____________ : to send to another country
5. ____________ : to express one's joy at a happy event, etc.
6. ____________ : to be present at
7. ____________ : to bring from another country
8. ____________ : to live and grow very well

단어공부 7일째

따라하기 단어를 세 번씩 따라 써보세요.

105 **conceal** [kənsíːl]	v. 숨기다, 은폐하다(= hide)
106 **transport** [trǽnspɔːrt] [-pɔ́ːrt]	v. 수송[운송]하다 ▶ transportation : n. 수송[운송] ; 수송[운송]수단
107 **refuse** [rifjúːz]	v. 거절[거부]하다(= turn down)
108 **admit** [ədmít]	v. ❶ 시인[인정]하다 ❷ 들여보내다(= let in) ▶ admission : n. 시인; 입장료
109 **allow** [əláu]	v. 허용하다
110 **comfort** [kʌ́mfərt]	v. 위로[위안]하다 n. 위로[위안]
111 **forgive** [fərgív]	v. 용서하다
112 **graduate** [grǽdʒuèit]	v. 졸업하다 ▶ graduation : n. 졸업(식)

연습문제 1 영어는 우리말로, 우리말은 영어로 써 보세요.

1. admit ________
2. allow ________
3. conceal ________
4. comfort ________
5. graduate ________
6. forgive ________
7. transport ________
8. refuse ________

1. 시인하다 ________
2. 허용하다 ________
3. 수송하다 ________
4. 졸업하다 ________
5. 숨기다 ________
6. 위로하다 ________
7. 거절하다 ________
8. 용서하다 ________

연습문제 2 문장에 알맞는 단어를 써 보세요.

1. 그는 내게 빚진 돈을 갚기를 거부했다.
   He ____________ to give me the money that he owed me.
2. 새 자동차들은 선편으로 대양을 건너 수송된다.
   The new automobiles are ____________ across the ocean by ship.
3. 여기서는 주차가 허용되지 않는다.
   You're not ____________ to park here.
4. 그들은 꽃병을 깼음을 시인했다.
   They ____________ that they had broken the vase.
5. 어머니한테는 아무것도 숨기려 하지 말아라.
   Don't try to ____________ anything from your mother.
6. 우리의 새 영어선생님은 작년에 대학을 졸업했다.
   Our new English teacher ____________ from college last year.
7. 그는 내가 자기에 대해 한 말 때문에 나를 결코 용서하지 않았다.
   He never ____________ me for what I said about him.
8. 나는 제인의 부친이 돌아가신 후 그녀를 위로하려고 노력했다.
   I tried to ____________ Jane after her father's death.

연습문제 3 영영풀이에 맞는 단어를 써 보세요.

1. ____________ : to ease someone in pain or worry
2. ____________ : to take goods and people from one place to another
3. ____________ : to agree that something is true
4. ____________ : to pardon, to excuse
5. ____________ : to get a degree from a university or college
6. ____________ : to let, to permit
7. ____________ : to hide something carefully
8. ____________ : to turn down

단어공부 8일째

따라하기 단어를 세 번씩 따라 써보세요.

113 **rob** [rɑb]	v. 강탈하다 ▶ robbery : n. 강도, 강탈		
114 **commute** [kəmjúːt]	v. 통근[통학]하다 ▶ commuter : n. 교외 통근자[통학생]		
115 **stir** [stəːr]	v. 휘젓다, 뒤섞다(= mix)		
116 **jog** [dʒɑg]	v. 천천히 달리다		
117 **flee** [fliː]	v. 도망치다, 달아나다(= run away)		
118 **hop** [hɑp]	v. ❶ 깡총 뛰다 ❷ 껑충 뛰어 넘다(= jump over)		
119 **behave** [bihéiv]	v. 행동하다 ▶ behavior : n. 행동(= conduct)		
120 **suck** [sʌk]	v. 빨다 ▶ sucker : n. 젖먹이		

연습문제 1 영어는 우리말로, 우리말은 영어로 써 보세요.

1. stir ______	1. 도망치다 ______
2. hop ______	2. 통근하다 ______
3. suck ______	3. 빨다 ______
4. behave ______	4. 강탈하다 ______
5. rob ______	5. 천천히 달리다 ______
6. flee ______	6. 행동하다 ______
7. jog ______	7. 깡총 뛰다 ______
8. commute ______	8. 휘젓다 ______

연습문제 2 문장에 알맞는 단어를 써 보세요.

1. 아버지는 매일 아침 운동삼아 공원에서 천천히 달리신다.
   My father ____________ in the park every morning for exercise.
2. 그녀는 빨리 식게 스프를 휘저었다.
   She ____________ her soup to quicken its cooling.
3. 토끼와 개구리는 깡충 뛴다.
   Rabbits and frogs ____________.
4. 우리 이웃들 중 많은 사람들이 매일 도시까지 기차로 통근한다.
   Many of our neighbors ____________ to the city every day by train.
5. 그 아이는 빨대로 사과주스를 빨아 마셨다.
   The child ____________ the apple juice through a straw.
6. 그들은 우리를 성인처럼 대우하고 우리들이 성인처럼 행동하기를 기대한다.
   They treat us like adults and expect us to ____________ as such.
7. 그는 돈과 옷을 모두 강탈당했다.
   He was ____________ of all his money and clothes.
8. 사자를 보자 겁먹은 사슴들은 들판에서 달아났다.
   The frightened deer ____________ from the field when they saw the lion.

연습문제 3 영영풀이에 맞는 단어를 써 보세요.

1. ____________ : to mix something by moving it around with a spoon, etc.
2. ____________ : to jump with both legs together
3. ____________ : to take something away from by force
4. ____________ : to act in a particular way
5. ____________ : to run away from
6. ____________ : to travel to and from one's work or school regularly
7. ____________ : to take liquid into the mouth
8. ____________ : to run at a slow pace

단어공부 8일째

따라하기 단어를 세 번씩 따라 써보세요.

121 **neglect** [niglékt]	v. ❶ 소홀히 하다 ❷ (부주의로) 잊다 n. 소홀함
122 **boast** [boust]	v. 자랑하다, 뽐내다
123 **delight** [diláit]	v. ❶ 즐겁게 하다 ❷ 즐거워 하다
124 **hire** [haiər]	v. ❶ 고용하다(= employ) ❷ 빌리다(= rent)
125 **afford** [əfɔ́ːrd]	v. ~할 여유가 있다
126 **relax** [rilǽks]	v. ❶ 긴장을 풀다 ❷ 편히 쉬다 ▶ relaxation : n. 휴식; 완화
127 **interest** [íntərist]	v. 흥미있게 하다 n. 흥미, 관심
128 **satisfy** [sǽtisfài]	v. 만족시키다 ▶ satisfaction : n. 만족

연습문제 1 영어는 우리말로, 우리말은 영어로 써 보세요.

1. boast ______	1. 즐겁게 하다 ______
2. hire ______	2. ~할 여유가 있다 ______
3. afford ______	3. 긴장을 풀다 ______
4. satisfy ______	4. 소홀히 하다 ______
5. neglect ______	5. 흥미있게 하다 ______
6. interest ______	6. 만족시키다 ______
7. relax ______	7. 고용하다 ______
8. delight ______	8. 자랑하다 ______

연습문제 2 문장에 알맞는 단어를 써 보세요.

1. 그들은 희소식을 들어 즐거웠다.
   They were ____________ to hear the good news.

2. 그녀는 하인을 고용할 여유가 없었다.
   She could not ____________ to hire servants.

3. 그는 자기가 가장 똑똑하다고 뽐냈다.
   He ____________ that he was smarter than everyone else.

4. 그는 흥미있는 CD 한 장을 샀다.
   He bought a CD that ____________ him.

5. 어머니는 내가 내 방을 치워 놓은 상태에 만족하지 않았다.
   My mother was not ____________ with the way I cleaned my room.

6. 그들은 임무를 소홀히 하여 질책을 받았다.
   They were scolded for ____________ their duties.

7. 일주일 휴가를 가면 긴장이 풀리겠는데.
   A week's holiday would really ____________ me.

8. 우리는 집을 칠하려고 두 사람을 고용했다.
   We ____________ two men to paint the house.

연습문제 3 영영풀이에 맞는 단어를 써 보세요.

1. ____________ : to praise oneself, to be proud of something
2. ____________ : to employ; to rent
3. ____________ : to make happy
4. ____________ : to ignore
5. ____________ : to lose stress
6. ____________ : to make happy, to bring joy to
7. ____________ : to be able to pay for something
8. ____________ : to make someone curious

단어공부 9일째

따라하기 단어를 세 번씩 따라 써보세요.

129 **chuckle** [tʃʌ́kl]	v. 낄낄 웃다 n. 낄낄 웃음
130 **tickle** [tíkl]	v. ❶ 간질이다 ❷ 즐겁게 해주다
131 **slip** [slip]	v. ❶ 미끄러지다 ❷ 살짝 ~하다
132 **bound** [baund]	v. 경계를 이루다 n. 경계선
133 **sow** [sou]	v. 씨를 뿌리다, 파종하다
134 **tear** [tɛə*r*]	v. 찢다
135 **sew** [sou]	v. 꿰매다, 깁다
136 **wear** [wɛə*r*]	v. ❶ (몸에) 착용하다 ❷ 써서 낡게(닳게) 하다

연습문제 1 영어는 우리말로, 우리말은 영어로 써 보세요.

1. tickle ______
2. sow ______
3. sew ______
4. wear ______
5. tear ______
6. chuckle ______
7. bound ______
8. slip ______

1. 경계를 이루다 ______
2. 간질이다 ______
3. 씨를 뿌리다 ______
4. 꿰매다 ______
5. 낄낄 웃다 ______
6. 착용하다 ______
7. 찢다 ______
8. 미끄러지다 ______

연습문제 2 | 문장에 알맞는 단어를 써 보세요.

1. 미국은 서쪽으로 태평양에 경계를 두고 있다.
The United States is ____________ on the west by the Pacific.

2. 그 여자는 빙판 보도에서 미끄러졌다.
The woman ____________ on the icy sidewalk.

3. 그녀는 그 봉투를 찢어 열었다.
She ____________ the envelope open.

4. 경찰은 검은 우비를 입고 있는 남자를 찾고 있다.
The police are looking for a man ____________ a black raincoat.

5. 그는 앉아서 낄낄거리며 만화를 읽고 있었다.
He sat reading the comic, ____________ to himself.

6. 뜯어진 소매를 꿰매세요.
Please ____________ the torn sleeve.

7. 농부는 내일 이 밭에 옥수수씨를 뿌릴 것이다.
The farmer will ____________ corn in this field tomorrow.

8. 그녀는 깃털로 나를 간질였다.
She ____________ me with a feather.

연습문제 3 | 영영풀이에 맞는 단어를 써 보세요.

1. ____________ : to form the boundary of
2. ____________ : to put together with a needle and thread
3. ____________ : to touch lightly to cause laughter, etc.
4. ____________ : to pull apart, often by force
5. ____________ : to have clothes on
6. ____________ : to plant seeds
7. ____________ : to fall or almost fall because of something
8. ____________ : to laugh softly

단어공부 9일째

따라하기 단어를 세 번씩 따라 써보세요.

137 **lick** [lik]	v. 핥다
138 **slide** [slaid]	v. ❶ 미끄러지다 ❷ 활주하다
139 **dress** [dres]	v. ❶ (옷을) 입다(= put on) ❷ (옷을) 입히다
140 **weave** [wiːv]	v. (실·천을) 짜다
141 **whirl** [(*h*)wəːrl]	v. 빙빙 돌다, 선회하다 n. 선회, 소용돌이
142 **steer** [stiə*r*]	v. 조종하다 n. 수송아지
143 **sink** [siŋk]	v. ❶ 침몰하다 ❷ 가라앉히다
144 **rescue** [réskjuː]	v. 구조하다 n. 구조

연습문제 1 영어는 우리말로, 우리말은 영어로 써 보세요.

1. dress ________
2. rescue ________
3. steer ________
4. weave ________
5. sink ________
6. lick ________
7. whirl ________
8. slide ________

1. (실·천을) 짜다 ________
2. 침몰하다 ________
3. 미끄러지다 ________
4. 구조하다 ________
5. 핥다 ________
6. (옷을) 입다 ________
7. 조종하다 ________
8. 빙빙 돌다 ________

연습문제 2 문장에 알맞는 단어를 써 보세요.

1. 나는 학교에 늦어 재빨리 옷을 입었다.
   I (got) ____________ quickly because I was late for school.
2. 카누는 구멍이 생기면 가라앉을 수 있다.
   The canoe could ____________ if it has a hole.
3. 나뭇잎들이 바람에 빙빙 돌았다.
   The leaves ____________ in the wind.
4. 그 고양이는 접시에 있는 크림을 핥았다.
   The cat ____________ cream from a dish.
5. 승객 전원이 침몰하는 배에서 구조되었다.
   All the passengers were ____________ from the sinking ship.
6. 그 젖은 비누 덩어리가 마루에 미끄러져 갔다.
   The wet bar of soap ____________ across the floor.
7. 수로안내인은 배를 부두로 조종했다.
   The pilot ____________ the ship to the dock.
8. 이 기계는 실을 짜서 천을 만든다.
   This machine ____________ yarn into cloth.

연습문제 3 영영풀이에 맞는 단어를 써 보세요.

1. ____________ : to go down into water
2. ____________ : to turn or rotate very quickly
3. ____________ : to move smoothly over ice, etc.
4. ____________ : to free from danger or evil
5. ____________ : to move your tongue across something
6. ____________ : to guide the course of a ship, etc.
7. ____________ : to put on
8. ____________ : to make threads into cloth by crossing them

단어공부 10일째

따라하기 단어를 세 번씩 따라 써보세요.

145 **float** [flout]	v. (물에) 뜨다
146 **swallow** [swálou]	v. 삼키다 n. 제비
147 **flow** [flou]	v. 흐르다 n. 흐름
148 **merge** [məːrdʒ]	v. 합병[통합]하다, 융합하다 ▶ merger : n. 합병
149 **note** [nout]	v. 주목하다, 유념하다 n. 메모, 짧은 편지; 주목
150 **celebrate** [séləbrèit]	v. (식·축전으로) 축하하다
151 **bump** [bʌmp]	v. 부딪치다, 충돌하다 n. 충돌; 혹; (길의) 융기
152 **shock** [ʃɑk]	v. 깜짝 놀라게 하다 n. 충격; 쇼크

연습문제 1 영어는 우리말로, 우리말은 영어로 써 보세요.

1. swallow	______	1. 흐르다	______
2. shock	______	2. 주목하다	______
3. celebrate	______	3. 부딪치다	______
4. bump	______	4. (물에) 뜨다	______
5. merge	______	5. 깜짝 놀라게 하다	______
6. note	______	6. 삼키다	______
7. float	______	7. 축하하다	______
8. flow	______	8. 합병하다	______

연습문제 2 문장에 알맞는 단어를 써 보세요.

1. 수영반에서 우리는 누워서 뜨는 법을 배운다.
   In swimming class we learn how to ____________ on our backs.
2. 물이 이 파이프들을 통해 흐른다.
   Water ____________ through these pipes.
3. 영화는 8시에 시작됨을 유념하십시오.
   Please ____________ that the movie starts at 8 o'clock.
4. 우리는 그의 돌연한 죽음에 모두 깜짝 놀랐다.
   We were all ____________ by his sudden death.
5. 두 차가 서로 부딪쳤다.
   The two cars ____________ each other.
6. 음식을 잘 씹으세요. 그렇지 않으면 삼킬 수 없을 거예요.
   Chew your food well or you won't be able to ____________ it.
7. 많은 사람들은 서로 선물을 교환하면서 성탄절을 축하한다.
   Many people ____________ Christmas by giving one another presents.
8. 그들은 두 회사를 합병했다.
   They ____________ the two companies.

연습문제 3 영영풀이에 맞는 단어를 써 보세요.

1. ____________ : to observe, to pay attention to
2. ____________ : to move like a liquid
3. ____________ : to cause someone to feel sudden surprise or fear
4. ____________ : to stay on top of a liquid
5. ____________ : to do something special to mark an event, etc.
6. ____________ : to take food or drink into the throat
7. ____________ : to combine or become combined
8. ____________ : to hit with force

단어공부 10일째

따라하기 단어를 세 번씩 따라 써보세요.

153 **sprout** [spraut]	v. 싹이 돋다, 싹이 돋게 하다 n. 새싹
154 **frighten** [fráitn]	v. 겁을 먹게 하다(= scare, terrify)
155 **freeze** [fri:z]	v. ❶ 얼다 ❷ 얼리다
156 **yell** [yel]	v. 고함치다 n. 고함소리
157 **pray** [prei]	v. 기원하다, 빌다 ▶ prayer : n. 기도, 기원
158 **spill** [spil]	v. ❶ 엎지르다 ❷ 흘러나오다
159 **wipe** [waip]	v. 닦다
160 **soak** [souk]	v. ❶ 적시다, 담그다 ❷ 잠기다, 젖다

연습문제 1 영어는 우리말로, 우리말은 영어로 써 보세요.

1. frighten ______
2. pray ______
3. sprout ______
4. wipe ______
5. soak ______
6. freeze ______
7. spill ______
8. yell ______

1. 닦다 ______
2. 고함치다 ______
3. 겁을 먹게 하다 ______
4. 적시다 ______
5. 엎지르다 ______
6. 싹이 돋다 ______
7. 얼다 ______
8. 기원하다 ______

연습문제 2 문장에 알맞는 단어를 써 보세요.

1. 형은 자기 자전거를 가져갔다고 화가 나서 나에게 고함쳤다.
   My brother got mad and ____________ at me for taking his bicycle.
2. 그 아이는 탁자 위에 우유를 엎질렀다.
   The child ____________ milk on the table.
3. 물은 얼면 얼음이 된다.
   When water ____________, it becomes ice.
4. 내가 심은 씨앗들이 방금 싹이 돋았다.
   The seeds that I planted have just ____________.
5. 그녀는 빨기 전에 옷들을 물에 담갔다.
   She ____________ the clothes before washing them.
6. 네가 접시를 닦으면 내가 그것들을 닦아 말릴게.
   If you wash the dishes, I will ____________ them dry.
7. 우리는 길잃은 아이가 무사히 돌아오기를 기원했다.
   We ____________ for the safe return of the lost child.
8. 요란한 폭발음이 모두를 겁먹게 했다.
   The loud explosion ____________ everyone.

연습문제 3 영영풀이에 맞는 단어를 써 보세요.

1. ____________ : to become ice or icy
2. ____________ : to make a request to a god or spirit
3. ____________ : to rub away dirt, water, etc.
4. ____________ : to put or be in water for a long time
5. ____________ : to cause liquid, etc. to flow out
6. ____________ : to shout very loudly
7. ____________ : to start to grow
8. ____________ : to cause great fear

단어 test 6~10일

A 알맞은 단어를 골라서 쓰시오.

appreciate	boil	delighted	transported	exports

1. Let's ____________ some water for coffee.
2. I ____________ your running these errands for me.
3. Brazil ____________ coffee to a lot of countries.
4. The new automobiles are ____________ across the ocean by ship.
5. They were ____________ to hear the good news.

B 빈칸에 들어갈 알맞은 단어를 고르시오.

1. Call the theater and ____________ three seats.
   a. transfer b. analyze c. reserve d. employ
2. Big cars ____________ a lot of fuel.
   a. spend b. consume c. preserve d. explore
3. I have to ____________ a club meeting this afternoon.
   a. enter b. attempt c. listen d. attend
4. Many of our neighbors ____________ to the city every day by train.
   a. take b. commute c. appear d. observe
5. They were scolded for ____________ their duties.
   a. neglecting b. establsihing c. serving d. marking

C 빈칸에 들어갈 단어의 알맞은 형태를 고르시오.

1. I (got) ____________ quickly because I was late for school.
   a. dressed b. dress c. dresser

2. They ____________ the two companies.
   a. merger b. merged c. mergence

3. We ____________ for the safe return of the lost child.
   a. prayed b. prayer c. praying

4. I always ____________ before going to bed.
   a. bath b. batheable c. bathe

5. Breakfast is ____________ between 8 and 10 a.m.
   a. served b. service c. server

D 다음 주어진 동사를 문맥에 맞게 고치시오.

1. The rain is (leak)____________ in through a crack in the roof.

2. We were (lure)____________ to the park by the sound of music.

3. We must (preserve)____________ our natural resources.

4. Chew your food well so it can be (digest)____________ properly.

5. Early explorers used to (navigate)____________ by the stars.

단어공부 11일째

따라하기 단어를 세 번씩 따라 써보세요.

161 **cure** [kjuər]	v. 치료하다 n. 치료법, 특효약
162 **rush** [rʌʃ]	v. 급히 하다 n. 돌진, 쇄도
163 **shut** [ʃʌt]	v. 닫다
164 **slam** [slæm]	v. ❶ 쾅 닫다 ❷ 털썩 내려놓다
165 **lock** [lɑk]	v. 자물쇠를 채우다(↔unlock) n. 자물쇠
166 **erupt** [irʌ́pt]	v. (화산이)폭발하다, 분화하다 ▶ eruption : n. (화산의)폭발, 분화
167 **glow** [glou]	v. ❶ 빨갛게 불타다 ❷ 빛나다 n. 백열
168 **glare** [glɛər]	v. 눈부시게 빛나다 n. 눈부신 빛

연습문제 1 영어는 우리말로, 우리말은 영어로 써 보세요.

1. shut ______
2. lock ______
3. glow ______
4. erupt ______
5. glare ______
6. cure ______
7. slam ______
8. rush ______

1. 쾅 닫다 ______
2. 눈부시게 빛나다 ______
3. 급히 하다 ______
4. (화산이)폭발하다 ______
5. 빨갛게 불타다 ______
6. 치료하다 ______
7. 자물쇠를 채우다 ______
8. 닫다 ______

연습문제 2 문장에 알맞는 단어를 써 보세요.

1. 우리는 추워서 창문을 닫았다.
We ____________ the window because it was cold.

2. 잊지말고 앞문을 잠궈라.
Be sure to ____________ the front door.

3. 서두르지 않으면 우린 늦는다.
We'll have to ____________ or we'll be late.

4. 화산이 폭발하여 주위 땅이 용암으로 덮혔다.
The volcano ____________ and covered the surrounding land with lava.

5. 해변에 햇살이 눈부시게 빛났다.
The sunlight ____________ at the beach.

6. 감기를 치료하려면 누워 쉬어야 한다.
To ____________ a cold you should stay in bed and rest.

7. 벽난로의 석탄들이 빨갛게 불탔다.
The coals in the fireplace ____________.

8. 그는 나가면서 문을 쾅 닫았다.
He ____________ the door as he left.

연습문제 3 영영풀이에 맞는 단어를 써 보세요.

1. ____________ : to close
2. ____________ : to shine strongly
3. ____________ : to make an illness, injury, etc. end
4. ____________ : to burst out
5. ____________ : to give off light, usually without a flame
6. ____________ : to move or do something quickly
7. ____________ : to close very hard
8. ____________ : to close something firmly with a key

단어공부 11일째

따라하기 단어를 세 번씩 따라 써보세요.

169 **reflect** [riflékt]	v. ❶ 반사하다 ❷ 반영하다
170 **scrub** [skrʌb]	v. 문지르다 n. 문지르기
171 **sense** [sens]	v. 느끼다, 감지하다 n. 감각, 지각
172 **melt** [melt]	v. ❶ 녹다 ❷ 녹이다
173 **control** [kəntróul]	v. ❶ 통제하다 ❷ 억제하다
174 **rest** [rest]	v. 쉬다 n. 휴식
175 **sign** [sain]	v. ❶ 신호하다 ❷ 서명하다 n. 표시, 신호; 기색, 징후
176 **associate** [əsóuʃièit]	v. ❶ 연상하다[관련짓다] ❷ 사귀다

연습문제 1 영어는 우리말로, 우리말은 영어로 써 보세요.

1. sense
2. control
3. sign
4. scrub
5. rest
6. associate
7. reflect
8. melt

1. 녹다
2. 문지르다
3. 연상하다
4. 반사하다
5. 신호하다
6. 통제하다
7. 쉬다
8. 느끼다

연습문제 2 | 문장에 알맞는 단어를 써 보세요.

1. 설탕 덩어리가 홍차에 녹았다.
The lump of sugar ____________ in the tea.

2. 피곤하면 중단하고 잠시 쉬어라.
If you're tired, stop and ____________ for a while.

3. 그녀는 따뜻한 비눗물로 부엌의 식탁을 문질렀다.
She ____________ the kitchen table with warm soapy water.

4. 그는 나에게 안으로 들어가라고 신호했다.
He ____________ for me to go inside.

5. 모래는 햇빛과 열을 반사한다.
Sand ____________ light and heat from the sun.

6. 나는 그가 집에 다시 와서 기뻐하고 있음을 느낄 수 있었다.
I could ____________ that he was glad to be back home.

7. 나는 늘 여름하면 해변가의 소풍을 연상한다.
I always ____________ summer with picnics at the beach.

8. 경찰이 교통을 통제하고 있었다.
The police were ____________ the traffic.

연습문제 3 | 영영풀이에 맞는 단어를 써 보세요.

1. ____________ : to wash by rubbing hard
2. ____________ : to limit something
3. ____________ : to connect in the mind
4. ____________ : to send sound or light back
5. ____________ : to come to know about by feeling, etc.
6. ____________ : to relax, to stop work
7. ____________ : to change to a liquid
8. ____________ : to give a signal

단어공부 12일째

따라하기 단어를 세 번씩 따라 써보세요.

177 **attach** [ətǽtʃ]	v. ❶ 붙이다 ❷ 애착을 갖게 하다
178 **consist** [kənsíst]	v. 이루어져 있다(= be made up of)
179 **compose** [kəmpóuz]	v. ❶ ~을 구성하다 ❷ (시 · 문장을) 짓다; 작곡하다
180 **comprise** [kəmpráiz]	v. ❶ ~을 포함하다 ❷ ~으로 이루어지다(= consist of)
181 **appoint** [əpɔ́int]	v. ❶ 지정하다 ❷ 임명하다
182 **excel** [iksél]	v. 능가하다, 뛰어나다(= surpass)
183 **develop** [divéləp]	v. ❶ 발달시키다 ❷ 개발하다
184 **cultivate** [kʌ́ltəvèit]	v. ❶ (논밭)을 갈다 ❷ 재배[양식]하다

연습문제 1 영어는 우리말로, 우리말은 영어로 써 보세요.

1. consist	1. ~을 구성하다
2. comprise	2. 지정하다
3. excel	3. 붙이다
4. attach	4. 발달시키다
5. cultivate	5. 능가하다
6. compose	6. 이루어져 있다
7. develop	7. 갈다; 재배 하다
8. appoint	8. ~을 포함하다

연습문제 2 문장에 알맞는 단어를 써 보세요.

1. 하와이주는 8개의 큰 섬과 많은 작은 섬들을 포함한다.
   The state of Hawaii _____________ eight main islands and many smaller ones.

2. 그는 화학과 스페인어에 뛰어나다.
   He _____________ at chemistry and Spanish.

3. 농부는 밭을 갈고 있었다.
   The farmer was _____________ his fields.

4. 못으로 벽에 그 표지를 붙이세요.
   _____________ the sign to the wall with nails.

5. 근육은 운동을 함으로써 발달시킬 수 있다.
   You can _____________ your muscles by exercising.

6. 일행은 5명의 멤버로 구성되었다.
   The party was _____________ of five members.

7. 우리는 파티의 장소와 시간을 정했다.
   We _____________ a place and time for the party.

8. 배심원단은 12명의 배심원으로 이루어져 있다.
   A jury _____________ of 12 jurors.

연습문제 3 영영풀이에 맞는 단어를 써 보세요.

1. _____________ : to do much better than others

2. _____________ : to tie together, to connect

3. _____________ : to name; to choose

4. _____________ : to prepare the land to grow crops, etc.

5. _____________ : to be made up of

6. _____________ : to include, to contain

7. _____________ : to make something by putting its parts together

8. _____________ : to grow

단어공부 12일째

따라하기 단어를 세 번씩 따라 써보세요.

185 **stun** [stʌn]	v. ❶ 실신시키다 ❷ 큰 충격을 주다(= shock)
186 **create** [kriéit]	v. 창조하다 ▶ creative : a. 창의적인
187 **arrange** [əréindʒ]	v. ❶ 정돈하다 ❷ 준비하다
188 **found** [faund]	v. 설립하다 ▶ foundation : n. 설립; 기초
189 **establish** [istǽbliʃ]	v. ❶ 세우다(= set up) ❷ 제정하다
190 **furnish** [fə́:rniʃ]	v. 제공하다, 공급하다(= provide)
191 **equip** [ikwíp]	v. (필요한 것을) 갖추게 하다 ▶ equipment : n. 장비
192 **sparkle** [spɑ́:rkl]	v. 번쩍이다, 번득이다 n. 번쩍임, 광채

연습문제 1 영어는 우리말로, 우리말은 영어로 써 보세요.

1. found ______
2. furnish ______
3. create ______
4. sparkle ______
5. stun ______
6. arrange ______
7. equip ______
8. establish ______

1. 갖추게 하다 ______
2. 정돈하다 ______
3. 번쩍이다 ______
4. 제공하다 ______
5. 세우다 ______
6. 실신시키다 ______
7. 설립하다 ______
8. 창조하다 ______

연습문제 2 문장에 알맞는 단어를 써 보세요.

1. 학생들은 과학클럽을 설립하려고 함께 일했다.
   The students worked together to ____________ a science club.

2. 그 책은 여러분들에게 한국전쟁에 관한 유용한 사실을 제공할 것이다.
   The book will ____________ you with useful facts about the Korean War.

3. 호수는 햇빛에 번쩍였다.
   The lake ____________ in the sunshine.

4. 그는 강타를 맞고 실신했다.
   He was ____________ by the heavy blow.

5. 서류들을 책상 위에 정돈하세요.
   ____________ the papers on the table.

6. 모든 사람은 평등하게 태어났다.
   All people are ____________ equal.

7. 그 배는 화재시에 이용될 소방 호스를 갖추고 있었다.
   The ship was ____________ with hoses to be used in case of fire.

8. 그 대학은 컴퓨터에 관심있는 학생들을 위한 새로운 강좌를 개설했다.
   The college ____________ a new course for students interested in computers.

연습문제 3 영영풀이에 맞는 단어를 써 보세요.

1. ____________ : to start something such as organization
2. ____________ : to shine brightly
3. ____________ : to make unconscious or senseless
4. ____________ : to provide, to give something
5. ____________ : to put in order
6. ____________ : to make; to give life or form to
7. ____________ : to set up
8. ____________ : to give someone all the things that are needed

단어공부 13일째

따라하기 단어를 세 번씩 따라 써보세요.

193 **polish** [páliʃ]	v. 닦다, 광을 내다 n. 광택, 광택제
194 **spread** [spred]	v. ❶ 퍼뜨리다 ❷ 퍼지다
195 **prepare** [pripέər]	v. 준비하다, 준비시키다 ▶ preparation : n. 준비
196 **contribute** [kəntríbjuːt]	v. ❶ 기여하다 ❷ 기부하다 ▶ contribution : n. 기여, 기부(금)
197 **decorate** [dékərèit]	v. 장식하다
198 **cooperate** [kouápərèit]	v. 협력하다
199 **stretch** [stretʃ]	v. 펴다, 뻗다
200 **extend** [iksténd]	v. (거리·기간을) 연장하다 ▶ extension : n. 연장; (진화의) 내선

연습문제 1 영어는 우리말로, 우리말은 영어로 써 보세요.

1. prepare ____	1. 장식하다 ____
2. cooperate ____	2. 연장하다 ____
3. spread ____	3. 펴다 ____
4. extend ____	4. 준비하다 ____
5. decorate ____	5. 닦다 ____
6. stretch ____	6. 협력하다 ____
7. polish ____	7. 기여하다 ____
8. contribute ____	8. 퍼뜨리다 ____

연습문제 2 문장에 알맞는 단어를 써 보세요.

1. 아이들은 크리스마스 트리를 등불로 장식했다.
The children ____________ the Christmas tree with lights.

2. 우리는 늘 비상시에 대비해야 한다.
We should always ____________ for an emergency.

3. 시는 그 길을 연장할 계획이다.
The city plans to ____________ the road.

4. 모두가 교실을 장식하는 데 협력했다.
Everyone ____________ in decorating the classroom.

5. 그들은 손님들이 오기 전 참나무 테이블을 광이 나게 닦았다.
They ____________ the oak table before the guests arrived.

6. 그녀는 쉬려고 침대 위에서 팔다리를 뻗었다.
She ____________ out on the bed to rest.

7. 내일 학교 수업이 없을 거라는 소문을 누가 퍼뜨렸나?
Who ____________ the rumor that school would be closed tomorrow?

8. 그는 이 도시의 발전에 기여했다.
He ____________ to the development of this city.

연습문제 3 영영풀이에 맞는 단어를 써 보세요.

1. ____________ : to make something longer
2. ____________ : to give money or help
3. ____________ : to rub something until it is smooth and shiny
4. ____________ : to act or work together
5. ____________ : to cover over a larger area or period of time
6. ____________ : to extend the body, etc. to the full length
7. ____________ : to make something ready
8. ____________ : to make something beautiful

단어공부 13일째

따라하기 단어를 세 번씩 따라 써보세요.

201 **swell** [swel]	v. 부풀다, 불어나다
202 **promote** [prəmóut]	v. ❶ 승진하다 ❷ 촉진하다 ▶ promotion : n. 승진, 촉진
203 **compare** [kəmpέər]	v. 비교하다 ▶ comparable : a. 필적하는
204 **devise** [diváiz]	v. 고안하다, 안출하다(= think up, invent)
205 **drag** [dræg]	v. 질질 끌다
206 **resemble** [rizémbl]	v. 닮다(= take after)
207 **block** [blɑk]	v. 막다, 방해하다
208 **prevent** [privént]	v. 방지하다, 막다

연습문제 1 영어는 우리말로, 우리말은 영어로 써 보세요.

1. resemble ______
2. promote ______
3. drag ______
4. prevent ______
5. compare ______
6. block ______
7. devise ______
8. swell ______

1. 비교하다 ______
2. 막다, 방해하다 ______
3. 닮다 ______
4. 부풀다 ______
5. 방지하다 ______
6. 질질 끌다 ______
7. 승진하다 ______
8. 고안하다 ______

연습문제 2 | 문장에 알맞는 단어를 써 보세요.

1. 그들은 아무도 해독할 수 없는 암호를 고안해냈다.
   They ____________ a secret code that no one could decipher.
2. 그녀의 목소리는 엄마를 닮았다.
   Her voice ____________ her mother's.
3. 그녀는 책임자로 승진되었다.
   She was ____________ to manager.
4. 그들은 옆 방으로 책상을 끌고 갔다.
   They ____________ the desk into the next room.
5. 창밖의 소음 때문에 한숨도 자지 못했다.
   The noise outside our window ____________ me from sleeping a wink.
6. 오늘의 생활비를 1년 전의 생활비와 비교해 보라.
   ____________ the living costs of today with those of last year.
7. 그의 다친 발목이 붓기 시작했다.
   His injured ankle began to ____________.
8. 높은 건물이 나의 방 창문의 시계(視界)를 막고 있다.
   A tall building ____________ the view from my window.

연습문제 3 | 영영풀이에 맞는 단어를 써 보세요.

1. ____________ : to look like someone or something else
2. ____________ : to examine what is different or similar
3. ____________ : to keep from happening
4. ____________ : to think up, to invent
5. ____________ : to stop something from moving
6. ____________ : to gradually increase in amount or number
7. ____________ : to pull something with difficulty
8. ____________ : to advance in rank, to give someone a better job

단어공부 14일째

따라하기 단어를 세 번씩 따라 써보세요.

209 **soar** [sɔːr]	v. 높이 날다, 치솟다 n. 비상, 높이 날기
210 **shift** [ʃift]	v. 이동하다, (위치를)변경하다 n. 이동
211 **stray** [strei]	v. 길을 잃다, 헤매다 a. 길 잃은
212 **remove** [rimúːv]	v. 제거하다(= get rid of), 치우다(= take away) ▶ removal : n. 제거
213 **bear** [bɛər]	v. ❶ (열매를)맺다, 낳다 ❷ 견디다, 참다(= stand, put up with)
214 **arise** [əráiz]	v. 발생하다, 일어나다(= come up)
215 **fix** [fiks]	v. ❶ 고치다(= mend) ❷ 고정시키다
216 **improve** [imprúːv]	v. 개선하다, 향상시키다

연습문제 1 영어는 우리말로, 우리말은 영어로 써 보세요.

1. fix ______
2. shift ______
3. bear ______
4. improve ______
5. remove ______
6. arise ______
7. soar ______
8. stray ______

1. 제거하다 ______
2. 발생하다 ______
3. 높이 날다 ______
4. 개선하다 ______
5. 길을 잃다 ______
6. 고치다 ______
7. 이동하다 ______
8. (열매를)맺다 ______

연습문제 2 | 문장에 알맞는 단어를 써 보세요.

1. 그 아이는 집을 나가 헤맸다.
The child ____________ from home.

2. 몇 가지 예기치 않은 일들이 일어났다.
Some unexpected events ____________.

3. 그들은 춤을 출 수 있게 양탄자를 치웠다.
They ____________ the rugs so they could dance.

4. 로켓은 궤도로 치솟았다.
The rocket ____________ into orbit.

5. 나는 영어실력을 향상시키려고 교습을 받고 있다.
I am taking lessons to ____________ my English.

6. 그 복숭아 나무에는 복숭아가 열린다.
The peach tree ____________ fruit.

7. 그림을 약간 오른쪽으로 이동하세요.
____________ the picture slightly to the right.

8. 그가 부서진 탁자를 고칠 것이다.
He will ____________ the broken table.

연습문제 3 | 영영풀이에 맞는 단어를 써 보세요.

1. ____________ : to give birth to
2. ____________ : to lose one's way
3. ____________ : to occur, to happen
4. ____________ : to fly high
5. ____________ : to make better
6. ____________ : to get rid of, to take away
7. ____________ : to change from one position to another
8. ____________ : to make something work properly

단어공부 14일째

따라하기 단어를 세 번씩 따라 써보세요.

217 **possess** [pəzés]	v. 소유하다(= own)
218 **limp** [limp]	v. 다리를 절다 n. 절름거림
219 **murmur** [mə́ːrmər]	v. ❶ 중얼거리다 ❷ 속삭이다
220 **owe** [ou]	v. ❶ 빚지고 있다 ❷ ~덕택이다
221 **pant** [pænt]	v. 헐떡거리다(= gasp) n. 헐떡거림
222 **match** [mætʃ]	v. ❶ 어울리다 ❷ 필적하다
223 **endure** [indúər]	v. 견디어내다 ▶ endurance : n. 인내
224 **repair** [ripέər]	v. (복잡한 것을)수리[수선]하다 n. 수리

연습문제 1 영어는 우리말로, 우리말은 영어로 써 보세요.

1. limp ______________
2. pant ______________
3. possess ______________
4. repair ______________
5. owe ______________
6. endure ______________
7. match ______________
8. murmur ______________

1. 중얼거리다 ______________
2. 어울리다 ______________
3. 소유하다 ______________
4. 빚지고 있다 ______________
5. 수리[수선]하다 ______________
6. 다리를 절다 ______________
7. 견디어내다 ______________
8. 헐떡거리다 ______________

연습문제 2 문장에 알맞는 단어를 써 보세요.

1. 나는 네가 자면서 중얼거리는 것을 들었다.
   I heard you ____________ in your sleep.

2. 경주가 끝난 후 주자들은 결승선에 서서 헐떡거리고 있었다.
   After the race, the runners stood ____________ at the finish line.

3. 북극의 최초 탐험가들은 많은 고난을 견뎌야 했다.
   The first explorers of the North Pole had to ____________ many hardships.

4. 그는 구두를 수선했다.
   He had his shoes ____________.

5. 그녀는 식료품점에 5달러의 외상이 있다.
   She ____________ five dollars to the grocery.

6. 아인슈타인은 굉장한 지성을 소유했다.
   Einstein ____________ great intelligence.

7. 나는 한 남자가 다리를 절며 길을 건너는 것을 보았다.
   I saw a man ____________ across the street.

8. 이 구두는 당신의 드레스에 잘 어울릴 것이다.
   These shoes would ____________ your dress nicely.

연습문제 3 영영풀이에 맞는 단어를 써 보세요.

1. ____________ : to fit, to suit

2. ____________ : to speak with a low tone

3. ____________ : to breathe hard and quickly

4. ____________ : to fix something

5. ____________ : to walk with difficulty

6. ____________ : to put up with pain, etc.

7. ____________ : to have something

8. ____________ : to be in debt to someone

단어공부 15일째

따라하기 단어를 세 번씩 따라 써보세요.

225 **stagger** [stǽgər]	v. 비틀거리다 n. 비틀거림
226 **replace** [ripléis]	v. 대신하다, 대체하다(= take the place of)
227 **wrap** [ræp]	v. 싸다, 포장하다
228 **recall** [rikɔ́ːl]	v. 상기하다, 생각해내다
229 **remind** [rimáind]	v. 상기시키다, 일깨우다
230 **whine** [wain]	v. 징징대다, 칭얼대다
231 **occur** [əkə́ːr]	v. 일어나다, 생기다(= take place)
232 **mend** [mend]	v. (간단한 것을) 수선하다

연습문제 1 영어는 우리말로, 우리말은 영어로 써 보세요.

1. wrap ______
2. occur ______
3. remind ______
4. stagger ______
5. mend ______
6. whine ______
7. replace ______
8. recall ______

1. 비틀거리다 ______
2. 상기하다 ______
3. 징징대다 ______
4. 대신하다 ______
5. 수선하다 ______
6. 상기시키다 ______
7. 일어나다 ______
8. 싸다 ______

연습문제 2 문장에 알맞는 단어를 써 보세요.

1. 파란 종이로 싼 이 꾸러미를 봐.
   Look at this package ____________ in blue.

2. 내가 잊지 않고 약을 복용하게 상기시켜 주세요.
   Please ____________ me to take my medicine.

3. 화재는 한밤중에 일어났다.
   The fire ____________ in the middle of the night.

4. 많은 근로자들이 컴퓨터로 대체되었다.
   Many workers have been ____________ by computers.

5. 나는 그 깨진 컵을 수선하려고 아교를 썼다.
   I used glue to ____________ the broken cup.

6. 그 취객은 길을 비틀거리며 갔다.
   The drunken man ____________ along the road.

7. 아기는 우리가 아무리 달래봐도 칭얼댔다.
   The baby ____________ no matter what we did for him.

8. 그의 얼굴은 낯익었지만 나는 그의 이름이 생각나지 않았다.
   His face was familiar, but I didn't ____________ his name.

연습문제 3 영영풀이에 맞는 단어를 써 보세요.

1. ____________ : to cover
2. ____________ : to make a long high unpleasant sound
3. ____________ : to take the place of something
4. ____________ : to repair, such as holes in fences or clothes
5. ____________ : to walk as if about to fall
6. ____________ : to cause someone to remember something
7. ____________ : to remember something
8. ____________ : to happen

단어공부 15일째

따라하기 단어를 세 번씩 따라 써보세요.

233 **punish** [pʌ́niʃ]	v. 벌주다, 처벌하다
234 **subtract** [səbtrǽkt]	v. 빼다(↔add) ▶ subtraction : n. 빼기(↔addition)
235 **emerge** [imə́ːrdʒ]	v. 나타나다, 출현하다
236 **fade** [feid]	v. ❶ (색깔이) 바래다 ❷ (소리·기억이) 서서히 사라지다
237 **starve** [stɑːrv]	v. 굶주리다, 굶어 죽다 ▶ starvation : n. 기아, 아사
238 **wander** [wɑ́ndər]	v. 떠돌다, 배회하다(= rove, roam)
239 **multiply** [mʌ́ltəplài]	v. ❶ 곱하다 ❷ 증가시키다 ▶ multiplication : n. 곱셈, 증가
240 **refund** [rifʌ́nd]	v. 환불하다 n. 환불

연습문제 1 영어는 우리말로, 우리말은 영어로 써 보세요.

1. multiply ______
2. refund ______
3. subtract ______
4. fade ______
5. wander ______
6. emerge ______
7. punish ______
8. starve ______

1. 나타나다 ______
2. 벌주다 ______
3. 곱하다 ______
4. 굶주리다 ______
5. 환불하다 ______
6. 빼다 ______
7. 떠돌다 ______
8. (색깔이) 바래다 ______

연습문제 2 문장에 알맞는 단어를 써 보세요.

1. 홍수가 지나고 나서 식량이 없었기 때문에 사람들은 굶주려야만 했다.
   The people had to ____________ because there was no food after the flood.

2. 태양이 구름 뒤에서 나타났다.
   The sun ____________ from behind a cloud.

3. 2에 5를 곱하면 10이 된다.
   If we ____________ 2 times 5, we get 10.

4. 만족하시지 않으면 귀하의 돈을 환불해드립니다.
   If you are not satisfied, your money will be ____________.

5. 선생님은 부정행위를 한 수잔을 벌주었다.
   The teacher ____________ Susan for cheating.

6. 청바지는 빨면 색이 바랠 수도 있다.
   Blue jeans may ____________ when they are washed.

7. 우리는 꽃들을 찾아 숲 속을 떠돌았다.
   We ____________ through the woods looking for flowers.

8. 7에서 3을 빼면 4가 남는다.
   ____________ 3 from 7, and you have 4.

연습문제 3 영영풀이에 맞는 단어를 써 보세요.

1. ____________ : to increase by a number of times
2. ____________ : to appear
3. ____________ : to cause someone to suffer for a crime
4. ____________ : to suffer or die from a lack of food
5. ____________ : to take away a number [amount] from another
6. ____________ : to lose the original color
7. ____________ : to give a money back
8. ____________ : to go from place to place without a clear purpose

단어 test 11~15일

A 알맞은 단어를 골라서 쓰시오.

comprises	cure	furnish	associate	established

1. To ____________ a cold you should stay in bed and rest.
2. I always ____________ summer with picnics at the beach.
3. The state of Hawaii ____________ eight main islands and many smaller ones.
4. The book will ____________ you with useful facts about the Korean War.
5. The college ____________ a new course for students interested in computers.

B 빈칸에 들어갈 알맞은 단어를 고르시오.

1. The children ____________ the Christmas tree with lights.
   a. painted b. decorated c. renovated d. cited
2. We should always ____________ for an emergency.
   a. guide b. direct c. exercise d. prepare
3. He ____________ to the development of this city.
   a. contributed b. supplied c. gave d. displayed
4. Her voice ____________ her mother's.
   a. resembles b. shows c. presents d. exposes
5. I am taking lessons to ____________ my English.
   a. reveal b. add c. improve d. worsen

C 빈칸에 들어갈 단어의 알맞은 형태를 고르시오.

1. Einstein ____________ great intelligence.
   a. possessed b. possession c. possessive

2. These shoes would ____________ your dress nicely.
   a. match b. matcher c. matching

3. The fire ____________ in the middle of the night.
   a. occurrence b. occurred c. occurrent

4. The sun ____________ from behind a cloud.
   a. emergency b. emergence c. emerged

5. Sand ____________ light and heat from the sun.
   a. reflects b. reflective c. reflection

D 다음 주어진 동사를 문맥에 맞게 고치시오.

1. He had his shoes (repair)____________.

2. (shift)____________ the picture slightly to the right.

3. He will (fix) ____________ the broken table.

4. I saw a man (limp) ____________ across the street.

5. If you are not satisfied, your money will be (refund) ____________.

단어공부 16일째

따라하기 단어를 세 번씩 따라 써보세요.

241 **overtake** [òuvərtéik]	v. 따라잡다(= catch up with)
242 **recycle** [rìːsáikl]	v. 재활용하다
243 **advertise** [ǽdvərtàiz]	v. 광고하다 ▶ advertisement : n. 광고
244 **calculate** [kǽlkjulèit]	v. 계산하다 ▶ calculation : n. 계산
245 **beg** [beg]	v. 간청하다
246 **lay** [lei]	v. 두다, 놓다(= put)
247 **realize** [ríəlàiz]	v. ❶ 깨닫다 ❷ 실현하다 ▶ realization : n. 인식; 실현
248 **check** [tʃek]	v. 확인하다, 조사하다 n. 수표; 계산서

연습문제 1 영어는 우리말로, 우리말은 영어로 써 보세요.

1. calculate ______	1. 광고하다 ______
2. overtake ______	2. 두다, 놓다 ______
3. lay ______	3. 따라잡다 ______
4. advertise ______	4. 확인하다 ______
5. realize ______	5. 간청하다 ______
6. check ______	6. 깨닫다 ______
7. recycle ______	7. 재활용하다 ______
8. beg ______	8. 계산하다 ______

연습문제 2 문장에 알맞는 단어를 써 보세요.

1. 제발 부탁하지만 거기에 혼자 가지 마라.
I ____________ you not to go there alone.

2. 그들은 신제품을 TV에 광고할 계획이다.
They are planning on ____________ their new product on TV.

3. 그는 친구를 따라잡으려고 빨리 달렸다.
He ran fast to ____________ his friend.

4. 그 때 가서야 비로소 우리는 그것의 중요성을 깨달았다.
Not until then did we ____________ its importance.

5. 내년에 우리가 필요한 돈이 얼마인지 계산하세요.
____________ how much money we will need next year.

6. 문이 모두 잠겼는지 잊지 말고 확인하라.
Don't forget to ____________ if the doors are all locked.

7. 우리 시는 깡통과 병을 재활용한다.
Our city ____________ cans and bottles.

8. 내 코트를 이 의자 위에 놓아도 되겠습니까?
May I ____________ my coat over this chair?

연습문제 3 영영풀이에 맞는 단어를 써 보세요.

1. ____________ : to do math (to add, subtract, etc.)
2. ____________ : to put down
3. ____________ : to treat used things to be used again
4. ____________ : to examine that something is in good order
5. ____________ : to put a notice in a newspaper, etc.
6. ____________ : to begin to understand
7. ____________ : to ask for something
8. ____________ : to catch up with

단어공부 16일째

따라하기 단어를 세 번씩 따라 써보세요.

249 **pop** [pɑp]	v. ❶ 펑 하며 터뜨리다[터지다] ❷ 불쑥 나타나다
250 **lean** [liːn]	v. ❶ 기대다 ❷ 기대게 하다
251 **tend** [tend]	v. ~하는 경향이 있다 ▶ tendency : n. 경향
252 **appeal** [əpíːl]	v. 매력이 있다(= be attractive), 마음에 들다
253 **exhaust** [igzɔ́ːst]	v. 기진맥진하게 하다 ▶ exhausted : a. 기진 맥진한; 고갈된
254 **tread** [tred]	v. 밟다
255 **spin** [spin]	v. (빠른 속도로)회전하다
256 **seize** [siːz]	v. (갑자기)붙잡다

연습문제 1 영어는 우리말로, 우리말은 영어로 써 보세요.

1. lean ____________
2. spin ____________
3. exhaust ____________
4. seize ____________
5. tread ____________
6. tend ____________
7. pop ____________
8. appeal ____________

1. 붙잡다 ____________
2. 기진맥진하게 하다 ____________
3. ~하는 경향이 있다 ____________
4. 밟다 ____________
5. 매력이 있다 ____________
6. 기대다 ____________
7. 회전하다 ____________
8. 펑 하며 터뜨리다 ____________

연습문제 2 문장에 알맞는 단어를 써 보세요.

1. 저 깨진 유리를 밟지 않도록 주의하세요.
Please be careful not to _____________ on that broken glass.

2. 그녀는 주말에 더 늦게 일어나는 경향이 있다.
She _____________ to get up later at the weekends.

3. 그녀는 갑자기 아이의 팔을 붙잡았다.
She _____________ the child by the arm.

4. 풍선을 터뜨리지 않도록 조심하라.
Be careful not to _____________ the balloon.

5. 오랫동안 수영을 해서 나는 기진맥진했다.
The long swim _____________ me.

6. 그 차의 바퀴가 진흙탕 속에서 빨리 돌았다(헛바퀴 돌았다).
The car's wheels _____________ in the mud.

7. 그는 벽에 기대어 있었다.
He was _____________ against the wall.

8. 이것은 모두의 마음에 드는 영화이다.
This is a movie that _____________ to everyone.

연습문제 3 영영풀이에 맞는 단어를 써 보세요.

1. _____________ : to bend over
2. _____________ : to attract; to please someone
3. _____________ : to take quickly by force
4. _____________ : to be apt, to incline
5. _____________ : to walk, to step
6. _____________ : to burst suddenly with a loud noise
7. _____________ : to turn around quickly
8. _____________ : to make very tired

단어공부 17일째

따라하기 단어를 세 번씩 따라 써보세요.

257 **snatch** [snætʃ]	v. 잡아 채다(= grab)
258 **grip** [grip]	v. ❶ 꽉 쥐다 ❷ (마음을)사로잡다
259 **flick** [flik]	v. (손가락으로)털어버리다
260 **obey** [oubéi]	v. 복종하다 ▶ obedience : n. 복종
261 **yield** [ji:ld]	v. ❶ 산출하다 ❷ 굴복하다(= give in to)
262 **spare** [spεər]	v. ❶ 아끼다 ❷ 할애하다 a. 여분의
263 **roam** [roum]	v. 돌아다니다, 배회하다(= rove)
264 **pursue** [pərsú:]	v. ❶ 추적하다 ❷ 추구하다 ▶ pursuit : n. 추적; 추구

연습문제 1 영어는 우리말로, 우리말은 영어로 써 보세요.

1. obey ______
2. grip ______
3. roam ______
4. yield ______
5. flick ______
6. pursue ______
7. snatch ______
8. spare ______

1. 아끼다 ______
2. 털어버리다 ______
3. 추적하다 ______
4. 잡아 채다 ______
5. 돌아다니다 ______
6. 산출하다 ______
7. 꽉 쥐다 ______
8. 복종하다 ______

연습문제 2 문장에 알맞는 단어를 써 보세요.

1. 그녀는 무릎에서 빵부스러기들을 털어버렸다.
   She ____________ the crumbs from her lap.

2. 최선을 다하려는 노력을 아끼지 말라.
   Don't ____________ any effort to do your best.

3. 겁먹은 아이는 어머니의 손을 꼭 잡았다.
   The frightened child ____________ his mother's hand.

4. 그들은 수 시간을 계속 거리를 배회하곤 했다.
   They used to ____________ the streets for hours on end.

5. 그녀는 나한테서 신문을 잡아채 갔다.
   She ____________ the newspaper from me.

6. 비옥한 토양은 풍작을 낳는다.
   Rich soil ____________ good crops.

7. 경찰은 도둑을 추적하여 길을 내려갔다.
   The police ____________ the thief down the street.

8. 그는 아버지의 말을 좀처럼 듣지 않았다.
   He seldom ____________ his father.

연습문제 3 영영풀이에 맞는 단어를 써 보세요.

1. ____________ : to do what is asked or ordered
2. ____________ : to not use all of something
3. ____________ : to hold firmly
4. ____________ : to grab quickly
5. ____________ : to chase, to go after someone to catch
6. ____________ : to give fruit, crops, etc.
7. ____________ : to move the hand or finger quickly
8. ____________ : to go freely over a large area

단어공부 17일째

따라하기 단어를 세 번씩 따라 써보세요.

265 **chase** [tʃeis]	v. 뒤쫓다, 추격하다 n. 추격
266 **aim** [eim]	v. 겨누다 n. 겨냥; 목표
267 **arrest** [ərést]	v. 체포하다 n. 체포
268 **patrol** [pətróul]	v. 순찰하다 n. 순찰(대)
269 **trace** [treis]	v. ~의 뒤를 밟다, 추적하다 n. 자취, 흔적
270 **postpone** [poustpóun]	v. 연기하다(= put off)
271 **attempt** [ətémpt]	v. 시도하다 n. 시도
272 **roar** [rɔːr]	v. ❶ (맹수가)포효하다 ❷ 고함치다 ❸ 굉음을 내다

연습문제 1 영어는 우리말로, 우리말은 영어로 써 보세요.

1. arrest ________	1. ~의 뒤를 밟다 ________
2. attempt ________	2. 체포하다 ________
3. aim ________	3. 시도하다 ________
4. patrol ________	4. 뒤쫓다 ________
5. roar ________	5. 연기하다 ________
6. chase ________	6. (맹수가)포효하다 ________
7. postpone ________	7. 겨누다 ________
8. trace ________	8. 순찰하다 ________

연습문제 2 문장에 알맞는 단어를 써 보세요.

1. 경찰은 도둑들의 은신처를 추적했다.
The police ____________ the thieves to their hiding place.

2. 그 죄수들은 탈출을 시도했다.
The prisoners ____________ an escape.

3. 움직이는 목표를 겨누기는 어렵다.
It is hard to ____________ at a moving target.

4. 그 사자는 우리 안에서 포효하고 있었다.
The lion was ____________ in his cage.

5. 그녀는 상점을 털었기 때문에 체포되었다.
She was ____________ for shoplifting.

6. 정보를 더 입수할 때까지 결정을 연기하자.
Let's ____________ making a decision until we have more information.

7. 사냥꾼들이 여우를 뒤쫓고 있다.
The hunters are ____________ a fox.

8. 시장은 순찰차를 증차하여 그 동네를 순찰케 하겠다고 약속했다.
The mayor promised that extra police cars would ____________ the neighborhood.

연습문제 3 영영풀이에 맞는 단어를 써 보세요.

1. ____________ : to put off
2. ____________ : to point a gun, etc. at
3. ____________ : to try to do something
4. ____________ : to find someone[something] after looking for them[it]
5. ____________ : to seize a person for illegal action
6. ____________ : to run or go after someone or something
7. ____________ : to make a deep, very loud sound
8. ____________ : to go around an area or building for guarding

단어공부 18일째

따라하기 단어를 세 번씩 따라 써보세요.

273 **growl** [graul]	v. 으르렁거리다 n. 으르렁거리는 소리
274 **grab** [græb]	v. 잡아채다(= snatch)
275 **sniff** [snif]	v. ❶ (코로) 들이마시다 ❷ (킁킁대며) 냄새를 맡다
276 **escape** [iskéip]	v. ❶ 탈출하다 ❷ 피하다, 면하다(= avoid)
277 **avoid** [əvɔ́id]	v. 피하다
278 **dare** [dɛər]	aux. 감히 ~하다
279 **resist** [rizíst]	v. 억제하다 ▸ resistance : n. 저항
280 **stain** [stein]	v. 더럽히다, 얼룩지게 하다 n. 얼룩, 때

연습문제 1 영어는 우리말로, 우리말은 영어로 써 보세요.

1. sniff ______	1. 탈출하다 ______
2. avoid ______	2. 억제하다 ______
3. stain ______	3. 잡아채다 ______
4. escape ______	4. 더럽히다 ______
5. resist ______	5. 으르렁거리다 ______
6. growl ______	6. 감히 ~하다 ______
7. dare ______	7. (코로)들이마시다 ______
8. grab ______	8. 피하다 ______

연습문제 2 문장에 알맞는 단어를 써 보세요.

1. 우리는 교통 혼잡을 피하려고 뒷길로 갔다.
We took a back road to ____________ the heavy traffic.

2. 우리는 맑은 산 공기를 들이마셨다.
We ____________ the clean mountain air.

3. 나는 그의 깃을 잡아챘다.
I ____________ him by the collar.

4. 네가 어찌 감히 그렇게 무례할 수 있느냐?
How ____________ you be so rude!

5. 내 셔츠에 잉크 얼룩이 졌어. 세제로 얼룩이 빠지면 좋겠는데.
My shirt is ____________ with ink. I hope the cleaner can remove it.

6. 그 개는 우체부에게 으르렁거렸다.
The dog ____________ at the mailman.

7. 나는 케이크를 한 조각 더 먹고 싶은 유혹을 참았다.
I ____________ the temptation to have another cake.

8. 네 명의 죄수들이 감옥에서 탈출했다.
Four prisoners ____________ from the jail.

연습문제 3 영영풀이에 맞는 단어를 써 보세요.

1. ____________ : to breathe in air with the nose (to smell)
2. ____________ : to make a low angry sound
3. ____________ : to have enough courage, nerve
4. ____________ : to not do something that you want to do
5. ____________ : to get free, to get away from
6. ____________ : to get a spot of color
7. ____________ : to stay away from
8. ____________ : to take something suddenly or roughly

단어공부 18일째

따라하기 단어를 세 번씩 따라 써보세요.

281 **scold** [skould]	v. 꾸짖다, 혼내다			
282 **blame** [bleim]	v. 탓하다, 나무라다(↔praise)			
283 **accuse** [əkjúːz]	v. ❶ 고발하다 ❷ 비난하다			
284 **announce** [ənáuns]	v. 발표[공표]하다 ▶ announcement : n. 발표, 공표			
285 **protest** [próutest] [-tést]	v. 항의하다 n. 항의(문)			
286 **search** [səːrtʃ]	v. 탐색하다, 수색하다 n. 수색, 탐색			
287 **condemn** [kəndém]	v. ❶ 비난하다 ❷ 유죄판결을 내리다			
288 **seek** [siːk]	v. ~을 찾다, 추구하다			

연습문제 1 영어는 우리말로, 우리말은 영어로 써 보세요.

1. accuse		1. 항의하다	
2. search		2. 탓하다	
3. seek		3. ~을 찾다	
4. blame		4. 고발하다	
5. condemn		5. 비난하다	
6. announce		6. 꾸짖다	
7. scold		7. 탐색하다	
8. protest		8. 발표하다	

연습문제 2 문장에 알맞는 단어를 써 보세요.

1. 그는 하천을 오염시킨 혐의로 고발되었다.
   He was ____________ of polluting the stream.

2. 고객들은 비싼 가격에 항의했다.
   The customers ____________ the high prices.

3. 많은 의사들은 흡연을 비난한다.
   Many doctors ____________ smoking.

4. 서툰 직공이 연장 탓을 한다.
   A bad workman ____________ his tools.

5. 찾아라, 그러면 주어질 것이니라.
   ____________ and you shall find.

6. 경찰은 행방불명된 아이를 찾으려고 그 지역을 수색했다.
   The police ____________ the area for the missing child.

7. 나는 그의 부주의를 꾸짖었다.
   I ____________ him for his carelessness.

8. 그는 갑자기 미국으로 떠난다고 발표했다.
   He suddenly ____________ that he was leaving for America.

연습문제 3 영영풀이에 맞는 단어를 써 보세요.

1. ____________ : to speak against; to object to[against]
2. ____________ : to charge with offense or crime
3. ____________ : to indicate strong disapproval of
4. ____________ : to find fault with or to chide
5. ____________ : to search for
6. ____________ : to hold responsible
7. ____________ : to look for something carefully
8. ____________ : to make something known publicly

단어공부 19일째

따라하기 단어를 세 번씩 따라 써보세요.

289 **wag** [wæg]	v. (꼬리를)흔들다			
290 **volunteer** [vɑ̀ləntíər]	v. 자원하다 n. 자원자			
291 **stumble** [stʌ́mbl]	v. 비틀거리다			
292 **graze** [greiz]	v. (가축이)풀을 뜯다			
293 **bare** [bɛər]	a. 벌거벗은			
294 **curious** [kjúəriəs]	a. 알고 싶어하는, 호기심 많은 ▶ curiosity : n. 호기심			
295 **jealous** [dʒéləs]	a. 질투하는 ▶ jealousy : n. 질투			
296 **immediate** [imíːdiət]	a. 즉각적인			

연습문제 1 영어는 우리말로, 우리말은 영어로 써 보세요.

1. stumble ______
2. curious ______
3. immediate ______
4. wag ______
5. graze ______
6. jealous ______
7. volunteer ______
8. bare ______

1. 벌거벗은 ______
2. 자원하다 ______
3. 풀을 뜯다 ______
4. 즉각적인 ______
5. (꼬리를)흔들다 ______
6. 알고 싶어하는 ______
7. 비틀거리다 ______
8. 질투하는 ______

연습문제 2 문장에 알맞는 단어를 써 보세요.

1. 그는 나무 뿌리에 걸려 비틀거렸다.
   He ____________ over the tree root.
2. 아이들은 모래밭을 맨발로 걸었다.
   The children walked on the sand with ____________ feet.
3. 그녀는 이웃의 행운에 질투심이 났다.
   She was ____________ of her neighbor's good fortune.
4. 그녀는 일을 끝내는 것을 도우려고 늦게까지 남겠다고 자원했다.
   She ____________ to stay late to help get the work finished.
5. 그 약은 병난 아이에게 즉각적인 효과가 있었다.
   The medicine had an ____________ effect on the sick child.
6. 그 강아지는 방문객들이 도착하자 꼬리를 흔들었다.
   The puppy ____________ its tail when the visitors arrived.
7. 그들은 무슨 일이 생길지 알고 싶어했다.
   They were ____________ to see what would happen.
8. 소들이 초원에서 풀을 뜯고 있었다.
   The cattle were ____________ in the meadow.

연습문제 3 영영풀이에 맞는 단어를 써 보세요.

1. ____________ : to trip or have trouble walking
2. ____________ : interested in knowing about things
3. ____________ : to shake up and down or move from side to side
4. ____________ : without delay, very near in time or place
5. ____________ : to agree to do something of one's own free will
6. ____________ : full of envy
7. ____________ : to feed on grass
8. ____________ : naked, nude

단어공부 19일째

따라하기 단어를 세 번씩 따라 써보세요.

297 **primitive** [prímətiv]	a. 원시적인
298 **instant** [ínstənt]	a. 즉시의, 즉각적인
299 **native** [néitiv]	a. ❶ 모국의 ❷ 토착의, 원산의 n. 토박이
300 **domestic** [dəméstik]	a. 국내의(↔foreign)
301 **tense** [tens]	a. 긴장한 ▶ tension : n. 긴장
302 **apt** [æpt]	a. ~하기 쉬운(=likely)
303 **tough** [tʌf]	a. ❶ 질긴(↔tender) ❷ 힘든(=difficult)
304 **marine** [məríːn]	a. 바다의

연습문제 1 영어는 우리말로, 우리말은 영어로 써 보세요.

1. domestic ______
2. instant ______
3. tough ______
4. native ______
5. marine ______
6. primitive ______
7. apt ______
8. tense ______

1. 모국의 ______
2. ~하기 쉬운 ______
3. 원시적인 ______
4. 긴장한 ______
5. 질긴 ______
6. 즉시의 ______
7. 바다의 ______
8. 국내의 ______

연습문제 2 문장에 알맞는 단어를 써 보세요.

1. 그는 외제품 보다는 국산품 구입을 더 좋아한다.
   He prefers to buy ____________ goods rather than foreign products.

2. 좀더 조심하지 않으면 다치기 쉽다.
   You are ____________ to hurt yourself if you are not more careful.

3. 한국은 그녀의 모국이다.
   Korea is her ____________ land.

4. 이 해안가에는 많은 종류의 바다 식물이 발견된다.
   Many kinds of ____________ life are found along this coast.

5. 원시인들은 종종 동굴에서 살았다.
   ____________ people often lived in caves.

6. 이 스테이크는 너무 질겨 좀처럼 씹을 수가 없다.
   This steak is so ____________ that I can hardly chew it.

7. 그 노래는 즉각 성공했다.
   The song was an ____________ success.

8. 그는 시험 전에 늘 긴장한다.
   He is always ____________ before an exam.

연습문제 3 영영풀이에 맞는 단어를 써 보세요.

1. ____________ : of one's own country

2. ____________ : likely, inclined

3. ____________ : immediate, happening at once

4. ____________ : hard and not easy to bite

5. ____________ : native, unchanged since ancient times

6. ____________ : of the sea

7. ____________ : of one's birthplace; inborn

8. ____________ : nervous and worried

단어공부 20일째

따라하기 단어를 세 번씩 따라 써보세요.

305 **individual** [indəvídʒuəl]	a. 개인의, 개개의 n. 개인
306 **toxic** [tάksik]	a. 유독한, 독성의(= poisonous)
307 **loose** [luːs]	a. ❶ 느슨한, 헐렁한(↔ tight) ❷ 풀려난 ▶ loosen : v. 느슨하게 하다, 풀어주다
308 **casual** [kǽʒuəl]	a. ❶ (의복)가벼운 차림의, 평상복의 ❷ 우연한
309 **particular** [pər*t*íkjulə*r*]	a. 각별한, 특별한(= special)
310 **normal** [nɔ́ː*r*məl]	a. 보통인, 정상적인
311 **ordinary** [ɔ́ː*r*dənèri]	a. 보통의, 평범한
312 **vital** [váitl]	a. 생명 유지에 필요한, 절대 필요한

연습문제 1 영어는 우리말로, 우리말은 영어로 써 보세요.

1. toxic ________	1. 보통인 ________
2. normal ________	2. 느슨한 ________
3. casual ________	3. 평범한 ________
4. ordinary ________	4. 개인의 ________
5. individual ________	5. 각별한 ________
6. vital ________	6. 절대 필요한 ________
7. loose ________	7. 유독한, 독성의 ________
8. particular ________	8. 평상복의 ________

연습문제 2 | 문장에 알맞는 단어를 써 보세요.

1. 이 책은 당신에게 각별한 흥미를 줄 것이다.
   This book should be of ____________ interest to you.

2. 그는 길고 헐렁한 코트를 입고 있었다.
   He wore a long, ____________ coat.

3. 네가 구운 이 빵은 보통 빵보다 훨씬 맛이 좋다.
   This bread you baked is much tastier than ____________ bread.

4. 우리는 여행에 관해 개개인의 견문록을 작성했다.
   We made ____________ reports on our trip.

5. 연중 이맘 때면 보통 폭우가 내린다.
   Heavy rain is ____________ at this time of year.

6. 폐는 생명을 유지하는 신체기관이다.
   The lungs are ____________ organs.

7. 저 공장들은 유독성 폐기물을 강에 버린다.
   Those factories dump ____________ wastes in the river.

8. 저녁식사에는 평상복을 입고 가도 된다.
   You may wear ____________ clothes to dinner.

연습문제 3 | 영영풀이에 맞는 단어를 써 보세요.

1. ____________ : informal, designed for wearing informally
2. ____________ : usual or expected
3. ____________ : not tight
4. ____________ : necessary for life, most important
5. ____________ : special or unusual
6. ____________ : different from others; single, separate
7. ____________ : usual
8. ____________ : poisonous; deadly

단어공부 20일째

따라하기 단어를 세 번씩 따라 써보세요.

313 **available** [əvéiləbl]	a. ❶ 입수[이용]할 수 있는 ❷ 바쁘지 않은
314 **convenient** [kənví:niənt]	a. 편리한(↔inconvenient)
315 **regular** [régjulər]	a. 규칙적인, 정기적인(↔irregular)
316 **accurate** [ǽkjurət]	a. 정확한(= exact, precise)
317 **plain** [plein]	a. ❶ 평이한, 쉬운 ❷ 명백한 n. 평야
318 **vague** [veig]	a. 막연한, 명확하지 않은(↔clear)
319 **mere** [miər]	a. 단순한, ~에 불과한 ▶ merely : ad. 단지
320 **private** [práivət]	a. ❶ 개인의 ❷ 비밀의, 비공개의

연습문제 1 영어는 우리말로, 우리말은 영어로 써 보세요.

1. convenient ________	1. 정확한 ________
2. mere ________	2. 막연한 ________
3. accurate ________	3. 편리한 ________
4. available ________	4. 단순한 ________
5. private ________	5. 규칙적인 ________
6. plain ________	6. 개인의 ________
7. regular ________	7. 입수할 수 있는 ________
8. vague ________	8. 평이한 ________

연습문제 2 문장에 알맞는 단어를 써 보세요.

1. 나는 이 곳의 단골 손님이다.
   I am a ____________ customer here.
2. 그의 길 안내가 좀 막연해서 우리는 길을 헤맸다.
   We got lost because his directions were rather ____________.
3. 좌석 있습니까?
   Are there any seats ____________?
4. 나는 개인적인 이유로 그것을 거절했다.
   I refused it for ____________ reasons.
5. 사건에 관한 그 신문기사는 정확하지 않았다.
   The newspaper stories about the accident were not ____________.
6. 당신에게 편리하시다면 저는 6시에 오겠습니다.
   If it is ____________ for you, I'll come at six.
7. 그것은 요행에 불과하다.
   It is ____________ good luck.
8. 글은 쉬운 영어로 써야 한다.
   You should write in ____________ English.

연습문제 3 영영풀이에 맞는 단어를 써 보세요.

1. ____________ : easy to see, hear, or understand
2. ____________ : happening or being at fixed times
3. ____________ : only; nothing more than
4. ____________ : easy and comfortable to do or get
5. ____________ : belonging to one person or group
6. ____________ : correct
7. ____________ : able to be used or possible to get
8. ____________ : unclear

단어 test 16~20일

A 알맞은 단어를 골라서 쓰시오.

exhausted	spare	arrested	primitive	leaning

1. ____________ people often lived in caves.
2. The long swim ____________ me.
3. He was ____________ against the wall.
4. Don't ____________ any effort to do your best.
5. She was ____________ for shoplifting.

B 빈칸에 들어갈 알맞은 단어를 고르시오.

1. The hunters are ____________ a fox.

   a. enhancing b. developing c. chasing d. advancing

2. The mayor promised that extra police cars would ____________ the neighborhood.

   a. move b. enjoy c. patrol d. play

3. Four prisoners ____________ from the jail.

   a. escaped b. avoided c. missed d. broke

4. A bad workman ____________ his tools.

   a. praises b. acclaims c. practices d. blames

5. ____________ and you shall find.

   a. Seek b. Admire c. Bless d. Cheer

C 빈칸에 들어갈 단어의 알맞은 형태를 고르시오.

1. He suddenly ____________ that he was leaving for America.
   a. announced　　b. announcement　　c. announcer

2. She was ____________ of her neighbor's good fortune.
   a. jealousy　　b. jealous　　c. jealously

3. They were ____________ to see what would happen.
   a. curious　　b. curiously　　c. curiosity

4. The song was an ____________ success.
   a. instance　　b. instant　　c. instantly

5. This book should be of ____________ interest to you.
   a. particularize　　b. particularity　　c. particular

D 다음 주어진 동사를 문맥에 맞게 고치시오.

1. They are planning on (advertise)____________ their new product on TV.

2. Not until then did we (realize)____________ its importance.

3. (calculate)____________ how much money we will need next year.

4. May I (lay)____________ my coat over this chair?

5. Don't forget to (check)____________ if the doors are all locked.

단어공부 21일째

따라하기 단어를 세 번씩 따라 써보세요.

321	**public** [pʌ́blik]	a. 공공의, 공무에 종사하는
322	**ample** [ǽmpl]	a. 충분한, 넉넉한(= sufficient)
323	**principal** [prínsəpəl]	a. 주요한, 으뜸가는(= main)
324	**splendid** [spléndid]	a. ❶ 호화로운 ❷ 멋있는(= excellent)
325	**major** [méidʒə*r*]	a. ❶ 대부분의 ❷ 중요한, 주요한
326	**minor** [máinə*r*]	a. (정도·중요성이) 적은, 경미한 n. 미성년자
327	**prime** [praim]	a. ❶ (가치·품질이) 최상의, 일류인 ❷ 주요한, 제1의
328	**bitter** [bítə*r*]	a. ❶ (맛이) 쓴 ❷ 지독한, 심한

연습문제 1 영어는 우리말로, 우리말은 영어로 써 보세요.

1. prime
2. public
3. splendid
4. minor
5. principal
6. major
7. bitter
8. ample

1. (중요성이) 적은
2. 주요한, 으뜸가는
3. 대부분의
4. 충분한
5. (맛이) 쓴
6. 공공의
7. (품질이) 최상의
8. 호화로운

연습문제 2 문장에 알맞는 단어를 써 보세요.

1. 금주 나의 주요 과제는 단어를 백 개 외우는 것이다.
   My ____________ task this weekend is to memorize 100 words.

2. 그의 용돈 중 대부분이 CD를 사는 데 들어갔다.
   The ____________ part of his allowance went to buy CDs.

3. 그들은 여비가 충분해 보인다.
   They seem to have ____________ money for the journey.

4. 그 진한 커피는 맛이 썼다.
   The strong coffee tasted ____________.

5. 우리는 그 정육점에서 최상급의 쇠고기를 구한다.
   We get ____________ beef from the butcher shop.

6. 공공의 해변은 누구든지 이용할 수 있다.
   A ____________ beach is for anybody to use.

7. 그 그림 멋진데.
   That's a ____________ painting.

8. 그는 머리에 경미한 부상을 입었다.
   He suffered a ____________ injury on the head.

연습문제 3 영영풀이에 맞는 단어를 써 보세요.

1. ____________ : great in size, importance or amount
2. ____________ : for the use of all people
3. ____________ : of the best quality
4. ____________ : main, most important
5. ____________ : having a sour, sharp taste
6. ____________ : more than enough
7. ____________ : excellent, wonderful
8. ____________ : small in size; of little importance

단어공부 21일째

따라하기 단어를 세 번씩 따라 써보세요.

329 **absolute** [ǽbsəlùːt]	a. 절대적인
330 **relative** [rélətiv]	a. 상대적인, 비교적인 n. 친척
331 **main** [mein]	a. 주된, 주요한(= principal, chief)
332 **sour** [sauər]	a. (맛이) 신
333 **pale** [peil]	a. ❶ 창백한 ❷ (색깔이) 엷은
334 **superior** [supíəriər]	a. 우월한 ▶ superiority : n. 우월
335 **inferior** [infíəriər]	a. 열등한; ~보다 (품질이) 떨어지는 ▶ inferiority : n. 열등
336 **junior** [dʒúːniər]	a. 손아래의(= younger), 연하의 n. 연소자

연습문제 1 영어는 우리말로, 우리말은 영어로 써 보세요.

1. junior ______
2. relative ______
3. sour ______
4. pale ______
5. inferior ______
6. absolute ______
7. superior ______
8. main ______

1. (맛이) 신 ______
2. 우월한 ______
3. 절대적인 ______
4. 손아래의 ______
5. 주된 ______
6. 상대적인 ______
7. 열등한 ______
8. 창백한 ______

연습문제 2 문장에 알맞는 단어를 써 보세요.

1. 우유 맛이 시큼해졌다.
   The milk has turned ____________.

2. 이 포도주는 내가 어제 마신 것보다 훨씬 우월하다.
   This wine is far ____________ to the one I had yesterday.

3. 일부 지배자들은 절대 권력을 갖고 있다.
   Some rulers have ____________ power.

4. 수퍼마켓의 대부분은 주요 도로에 있다.
   Most of the supermarkets are on the ____________ street.

5. 그는 나보다 두 살 아래다.
   He is two years ____________ to me.

6. 그녀의 가족들은 비교적 안락한 생활을 한다.
   Her family lives in ____________ comfort.

7. 그의 두 번째 소설은 첫 번째 보다 못하다.
   His second novel is ____________ to the first.

8. 그녀는 그 소식을 듣고 얼굴이 창백해졌다.
   She turned ____________ at the news.

연습문제 3 영영풀이에 맞는 단어를 써 보세요.

1. ____________ : the most important or largest
2. ____________ : having very little color
3. ____________ : lower in quality, value, etc.
4. ____________ : not limited; complete
5. ____________ : younger
6. ____________ : comparative
7. ____________ : having a taste like vinegar
8. ____________ : higher or better in quality, value, etc.

단어공부 22일째

따라하기 단어를 세 번씩 따라 써보세요.

337	**senior** [síːnjər]	a. 손위의, 연상의(= older)
338	**primary** [práimeri]	a. ❶ 주요한 ❷ 최초의
339	**due** [duː]	a. ❶ ~할 예정인 ❷ ~때문인(= because of)
340	**local** [lóukəl]	a. (특정) 지역의, 현지의
341	**sole** [soul]	a. 유일한
342	**universal** [jùːnəvə́ːrsəl]	a. ❶ 전세계의 ❷ 보편적인, 일반적인 ▶ universe : n. 우주; (the ~) 전세계
343	**brisk** [brisk]	a. 활발한, 기운찬(= energetic)
344	**similar** [símələr]	a. 비슷한, 유사한 ▶ similarity : n. 유사성

연습문제 1 영어는 우리말로, 우리말은 영어로 써 보세요.

1. universal ________
2. senior ________
3. sole ________
4. similar ________
5. primary ________
6. brisk ________
7. due ________
8. local ________

1. 전세계의 ________
2. (특정) 지역의 ________
3. 비슷한 ________
4. 주요한; 최초의 ________
5. 활발한 ________
6. 손위의 ________
7. 유일한 ________
8. ~할 예정인 ________

연습문제 2 | 문장에 알맞는 단어를 써 보세요.

1. 저 두 사람이 그 화재에서 살아남은 유일한 생존자들이었다.
   Those two people were the ____________ survivors of the fire.

2. 그는 매일 아침 활발히 산보하기를 좋아한다.
   He likes to take a ____________ walk every morning.

3. 비행기는 3시에 도착할 예정이다.
   The plane is ____________ to arrive at 3 o'clock.

4. 그는 그의 동생보다 7살 위였다.
   He was ____________ to his brother by seven years.

5. 이 두 모자는 너무 비슷해 구별하기가 어렵다.
   These two caps are so ____________ that it's hard to tell them apart.

6. 그가 공부하는 주된 이유는 더 좋은 일자리를 찾는 데 있다.
   His ____________ reason for studying is to get a better job.

7. 질병과 빈곤은 전세계적인 문제들이다.
   Disease and poverty are ____________ problems.

8. 우리가 도착하면 현지 시각으로 오전 1시가 될 것이다.
   It will be 1 a.m. ____________ time when we land.

연습문제 3 | 영영풀이에 맞는 단어를 써 보세요.

1. ____________ : only, single
2. ____________ : about or having to do with an area
3. ____________ : quick and active
4. ____________ : expected to arrive
5. ____________ : older than someone
6. ____________ : like something else but not exactly the same
7. ____________ : main, greatest
8. ____________ : of[for] all people; general

단어공부 22일째

따라하기 단어를 세 번씩 따라 써보세요.

345 **capable** [kéipəbl]	a. 유능한 ▶ capability : n. 능력
346 **bold** [bould]	a. 대담한(= brave)
347 **central** [séntrəl]	a. ❶ 중심에 있는 ❷ 중심적인, 주된(= main)
348 **grand** [grænd]	a. ❶ 웅대한 ❷ 성대한
349 **bald** [bɔːld]	a. 대머리의, 벗겨진
350 **enjoyable** [indʒɔ́iəbl]	a. 유쾌한, 즐거운(= pleasant)
351 **billion** [bíljən]	a. 십억의 n. 십억
352 **punctual** [pʌ́ŋtʃuəl]	a. 시간을 엄수하는(= on time)

연습문제 1 영어는 우리말로, 우리말은 영어로 써 보세요.

1. bold ________
2. enjoyable ________
3. grand ________
4. billion ________
5. capable ________
6. bald ________
7. punctual ________
8. central ________

1. 시간을 엄수하는 ________
2. 중심에 있는 ________
3. 유쾌한 ________
4. 유능한 ________
5. 대머리의 ________
6. 십억의 ________
7. 대담한 ________
8. 웅대한 ________

연습문제 2 문장에 알맞는 단어를 써 보세요.

1. 여러분들은 여기서 백두산의 웅대한 광경을 보실 수 있습니다.
You can enjoy a _____________ view of Mount Baekdu from here.

2. 그는 혼자서 적에 맞설 정도로 대담했다.
He was _____________ enough to face the enemy alone.

3. 강에 다리를 놓는 데 수십억 달러가 들었다.
Building the bridge across the river cost _____________ of dollars.

4. 나의 삼촌은 젊은데도 머리가 빠지고 있다.
My uncle is going _____________ even though he's young.

5. 유능한 기능공은 많은 것들을 고칠 수 있다.
A _____________ mechanic can fix many things.

6. 나는 늘 약속 시간을 지키려고 노력한다.
I always try to be _____________ for appointments.

7. 버스 터미널은 그 시의 중심부에 있다.
The bus terminal is in the _____________ area of the city.

8. 우리는 파티에서 즐거운 시간을 보냈다.
We had an _____________ time at the party.

연습문제 3 영영풀이에 맞는 단어를 써 보세요.

1. _____________ : giving joy, pleasant

2. _____________ : having the ability or power to do something

3. _____________ : with little or no hair on the head

4. _____________ : arriving or leaving on time

5. _____________ : very large and fine

6. _____________ : a thousand million

7. _____________ : of the center

8. _____________ : brave, willing to take risks

단어공부 23일째

따라하기 단어를 세 번씩 따라 써보세요.

353 **sound** [saund]	a. 건전한, 건강한(↔unsound)
354 **rare** [rɛər]	a. ❶ 매우 드문 ❷ 희박한 ▶ rarely : ad. 좀처럼 ~않다
355 **precious** [préʃəs]	a. 귀중한, 소중한
356 **pure** [pjuər]	a. 순수한(↔impure), 맑은 ▶ purity : n. 순수
357 **critical** [krítikəl]	a. ❶ 위급한, 중대한 ❷ 비판적인
358 **cunning** [kʌ́niŋ]	a. 교활한, 약삭빠른(=sly)
359 **constant** [kɑ́nstənt]	a. ❶ 변함없는 ❷ 끊임없는
360 **ideal** [aidíːəl]	a. 이상적인

연습문제 1 영어는 우리말로, 우리말은 영어로 써 보세요.

1. constant ____________
2. sound ____________
3. critical ____________
4. cunning ____________
5. pure ____________
6. rare ____________
7. ideal ____________
8. precious ____________

1. 교활한 ____________
2. 매우 드문 ____________
3. 이상적인 ____________
4. 귀중한 ____________
5. 변함없는 ____________
6. 순수한 ____________
7. 건전한 ____________
8. 위급한 ____________

연습문제 2 문장에 알맞는 단어를 써 보세요.

1. 그 환자는 위독한 상태이다.
   The patient is in a ____________ condition.

2. 금은 귀금속이다.
   Gold is a ____________ metal.

3. 여기는 젊은 부부에게 이상적인 집이 될 것이다.
   This will be an ____________ home for a young couple.

4. 흰코끼리는 매우 드문 동물이다.
   A white elephant is a ____________ animal.

5. 그렇게 변함없는 친구들이 있으니 너는 운이 좋다.
   You are lucky to have such ____________ friends.

6. 산에 오르자 공기는 더욱 맑아지고 선선해졌다.
   The air became ____________ and cooler as we climbed.

7. 그는 여우처럼 교활하다.
   He's as ____________ as a fox.

8. 건전한 정신은 건전한 신체에 깃든다.
   A ____________ mind in a ____________ body.

연습문제 3 영영풀이에 맞는 단어를 써 보세요.

1. ____________ : not mixed
2. ____________ : perfect; the best possible
3. ____________ : not common; not usual; not often
4. ____________ : clever
5. ____________ : valuable
6. ____________ : healthy or strong
7. ____________ : of crisis; very important
8. ____________ : staying the same; happening all the time

단어공부 23일째

따라하기 단어를 세 번씩 따라 써보세요.

361 **naughty** [nɔ́:ti]	a. 장난꾸러기인, 개구장이인
362 **noble** [nóubl]	a. ❶ 숭고한, 고상한 ❷ 고귀한, 귀족의
363 **fair** [fɛə*r*]	a. 공평한, 공정한(↔unfair)
364 **evil** [í:vəl]	a. 사악한(=wicked) n. 악, 악행
365 **pious** [páiəs]	a. 경건한(↔impious) ▸ piety : n. 경건
366 **firm** [fə:*r*m]	a. 굳은, 확고한 n. 회사
367 **strict** [strikt]	a. 엄격한, 엄한
368 **ashamed** [əʃéimd]	a. 부끄러워하는

연습문제 1 영어는 우리말로, 우리말은 영어로 써 보세요.

1. pious ____________
2. naughty ____________
3. strict ____________
4. fair ____________
5. evil ____________
6. ashamed ____________
7. noble ____________
8. firm ____________

1. 공평한 ____________
2. 부끄러워하는 ____________
3. 경건한 ____________
4. 숭고한 ____________
5. 엄격한 ____________
6. 장난꾸러기인 ____________
7. 굳은 ____________
8. 사악한 ____________

연습문제 2 문장에 알맞는 단어를 써 보세요.

1. 그 경건한 부부는 매일 교회에 나갔다.
The ____________ couple went to church every day.

2. 그들은 자녀들에게 매우 엄격하다.
They are very ____________ with their children.

3. 그 죄수는 공정한 재판을 받았다.
The prisoner was given a ____________ trial.

4. 그는 가난을 부끄러워했다.
He felt ____________ of being poor.

5. 가난한 사람들을 돕기 위해 최선을 다하는 것은 숭고한 행동이다.
It is a ____________ thing to do your best to help the poor.

6. 그 범인은 사악한 생활을 했다.
The criminal led an ____________ life.

7. 그들의 우정은 오랫동안 확고했다.
They had a ____________ friendship for many years.

8. 그는 반에서 장난이 심한 아이들 중 하나이다.
He's one of the ____________ children in the class.

연습문제 3 영영풀이에 맞는 단어를 써 보세요.

1. ____________ : just; honest

2. ____________ : demanding that rules should be obeyed

3. ____________ : showing love and duty to God and religion

4. ____________ : great and pure in mind; of high birth or rank

5. ____________ : feeling shame

6. ____________ : not easily moved or changed

7. ____________ : not good; very bad

8. ____________ : behaving badly

단어공부 24일째

따라하기 단어를 세 번씩 따라 써보세요.

369 **familiar** [fəmíljər]	a. ❶ 잘 아는, 정통한 ❷ 친숙한
370 **shameful** [ʃéimfəl]	a. 부끄러운, 창피스러운(= disgraceful)
371 **severe** [sivíər]	a. ❶ 가혹한, 심한 ❷ 혹독한
372 **upset** [ʌpsét]	a. 언짢은, 심란한 v. 언짢게 하다
373 **keen** [kiːn]	a. ❶ 열심인, 열중하는(= eager) ❷ 날카로운, 예민한
374 **innocent** [ínəsənt]	a. ❶ 무죄의, 결백한 ❷ 악의 없는, 천진난만한
375 **guilty** [gílti]	a. 유죄의 ▶ guilt : n. 유죄; 죄책감
376 **handy** [hǽndi]	a. ❶ 곁에 있는 ❷ 편리한

연습문제 1 영어는 우리말로, 우리말은 영어로 써 보세요.

1. familiar ____________
2. handy ____________
3. upset ____________
4. guilty ____________
5. shameful ____________
6. keen ____________
7. severe ____________
8. innocent ____________

1. 가혹한 ____________
2. 무죄의 ____________
3. 잘 아는 ____________
4. 곁에 있는 ____________
5. 열심인 ____________
6. 부끄러운 ____________
7. 유죄의 ____________
8. 언짢은 ____________

연습문제 2 문장에 알맞는 단어를 써 보세요.

1. 배심원단은 그녀에게 살인죄가 있다는 평결을 내렸다.
   The jury found her ____________ of murder.
2. 그는 모든 종류의 스포츠에 열심이다.
   He is ____________ about sports of all kinds.
3. 그가 거짓말을 한 것은 창피스러운 일이었다.
   It was ____________ of him to lie.
4. 그녀는 그가 편지를 해주지 않아 언짢았다.
   She was ____________ that he hadn't written.
5. 늘 사전을 곁에 두세요.
   Always keep a dictionary ____________.
6. 그가 이 범죄로부터 절대 결백함을 나는 확신한다.
   I'm sure he's absolutely ____________ of this crime.
7. 나는 이 지역의 길들을 잘 안다.
   I am ____________ with the roads here.
8. 그 남자는 가혹한 벌을 받았다.
   The man was given a ____________ punishment.

연습문제 3 영영풀이에 맞는 단어를 써 보세요.

1. ____________ : hard; very bad
2. ____________ : not guilty of a crime
3. ____________ : bringing or deserving shame
4. ____________ : having broken a law
5. ____________ : eager; willing
6. ____________ : well-known, seen often
7. ____________ : feeling unhappy
8. ____________ : easy to use

단어공부 24일째

따라하기 단어를 세 번씩 따라 써보세요.

377 **calm** [kɑːm]	a. ❶ 평온한(= peaceful) ❷ 침착한
378 **shy** [ʃai]	a. 수줍어하는(= bashful)
379 **anxious** [ǽŋkʃəs]	a. ❶ 걱정하는(= worried) ❷ 갈망하는(= eager) ▶ anxiety : n. 걱정; 갈망
380 **alike** [əláik]	a. 서로 닮은, 엇비슷한 ad. 똑같이
381 **extra** [ékstrə]	a. 여분의, 가외의(= additional)
382 **fluent** [flúːənt]	a. 유창한 ▶ fluency : n. 유창
383 **excess** [ékses]	a. 초과하는, 과잉의 n. 초과, 과잉 ▶ exceed : v. 초과하다
384 **lame** [leim]	a. 절름발이의, 불구의 v. 절름발이로 만들다

연습문제 1 영어는 우리말로, 우리말은 영어로 써 보세요.

1. alike	______	1. 초과하는	______
2. extra	______	2. 걱정하는	______
3. shy	______	3. 유창한	______
4. excess	______	4. 절름발이의	______
5. anxious	______	5. 서로 닮은	______
6. lame	______	6. 평온한	______
7. fluent	______	7. 여분의	______
8. calm	______	8. 수줍어하는	______

연습문제 2 문장에 알맞는 단어를 써 보세요.

1. 똑같은 지문을 가진 사람은 없다.
   No two people have fingerprints that are exactly ____________.

2. 그는 왼쪽 다리를 전다.
   He is ____________ in the left leg.

3. 그녀는 영어를 유창하게 한다.
   She is a ____________ speaker of English.

4. 그는 시험 결과에 대해 걱정하고 있다.
   He is ____________ about the results of the examination.

5. 바람 한 점 없이 평온한 아침이었다.
   It was a ____________ morning with no wind.

6. 잊지 말고 여분의 물을 갖고 가세요.
   Remember to carry ____________ water.

7. 항공편 여행일 경우 한도를 초과하는 짐에 대해 요금을 내야 한다.
   When you travel on an airplane, you have to pay for ____________ luggage.

8. 그 수줍은 어린이는 방으로 들어오려 하지 않았다.
   The ____________ little child wouldn't come into the room.

연습문제 3 영영풀이에 맞는 단어를 써 보세요.

1. ____________ : able to easily speak or write a language
2. ____________ : not liking to talk to people, esp. strangers
3. ____________ : very similar
4. ____________ : more than usual
5. ____________ : more than is needed
6. ____________ : quiet, peaceful
7. ____________ : worried, nervously fearful
8. ____________ : unable to walk easily because of some injury, etc.

단어공부 25일째

따라하기 단어를 세 번씩 따라 써보세요.

385 **greedy** [grí:di]	a. 탐욕스러운 ▶ greed : n. 탐욕
386 **loyal** [lɔ́iəl]	a. 충성스러운, 충실[성실]한 ▶ loyalty : n. 충성, 성실
387 **royal** [rɔ́iəl]	a. 왕의, 왕실의 ▶ royalty : n. 왕족, 왕실 사람들
388 **tropical** [trɑ́pikəl]	a. 열대 지방의 ▶ the tropics : 열대 지방
389 **temperate** [témpərət]	a. (기후가)온화한, 따뜻한
390 **mortal** [mɔ́:rtl]	a. 죽을 운명의, 필멸의(↔immortal)
391 **shallow** [ʃǽlou]	a. 얕은(↔deep)
392 **solar** [sóulər]	a. 태양의

연습문제 1 영어는 우리말로, 우리말은 영어로 써 보세요.

1. temperate ________
2. loyal ________
3. mortal ________
4. solar ________
5. royal ________
6. shallow ________
7. greedy ________
8. tropical ________

1. 충성스러운 ________
2. 죽을 운명의 ________
3. 열대 지방의 ________
4. 태양의 ________
5. 온화한 ________
6. 탐욕스러운 ________
7. 얕은 ________
8. 왕의 ________

연습문제 2 | 문장에 알맞는 단어를 써 보세요.

1. 미국의 대부분 지역은 기후가 온화하다.
Most areas of the United States have a ____________ climate.

2. 강은 얕아서 우리는 쉽게 바닥에 발이 닿을 수 있었다.
The river was ____________, so we could easily touch the bottom.

3. 그 옛 친구들은 서로에게 충실했다.
The old friends were ____________ to each other.

4. 원숭이는 대부분 열대 삼림지대에 서식한다.
Most monkeys live in ____________ forests.

5. 태양에너지는 때때로 가옥 난방에 이용된다.
____________ energy is sometimes used to heat homes.

6. 사람들은 부유해지면 질수록 탐욕스러워진다.
People get ____________ as they get richer.

7. 인간은 필멸의 존재로 반드시 죽는다.
Humans are ____________ beings and must die.

8. 왕실 가문은 궁전에서 산다.
The ____________ family lives in the palace.

연습문제 3 | 영영풀이에 맞는 단어를 써 보세요.

1. ____________ : of hot countries

2. ____________ : that must die

3. ____________ : wanting more than a fair share

4. ____________ : moderate in temperature

5. ____________ : not deep

6. ____________ : true and faithful

7. ____________ : like a king or queen

8. ____________ : of the sun

단어공부 25일째

따라하기 단어를 세 번씩 따라 써보세요.

393 **lunar** [lú:nər]	a. 달의	______	______	______
394 **sticky** [stíki]	a. 끈적거리는	______	______	______
395 **dim** [dim]	a. ❶ 어둠침침한(↔bright) ❷ 희미한	______	______	______
396 **cute** [kju:t]	a. 작고 예쁜, 귀여운	______	______	______
397 **sore** [sɔ:r]	a. 아픈(=painful)	______	______	______
398 **slender** [sléndər]	a. 날씬한(=slim)	______	______	______
399 **nearby** [níərbài]	a. 바로 가까이의 ad. 바로 가까이에	______	______	______
400 **voluntary** [vɑ́ləntèri]	a. 자발적인, 자원한	______	______	______

연습문제 1 영어는 우리말로, 우리말은 영어로 써 보세요.

1. cute	______	1. 날씬한	______
2. nearby	______	2. 어둠침침한	______
3. lunar	______	3. 바로 가까이의	______
4. voluntary	______	4. 작고 예쁜	______
5. dim	______	5. 달의	______
6. slender	______	6. 자발적인	______
7. sore	______	7. 끈적거리는	______
8. sticky	______	8. 아픈	______

연습문제 2 문장에 알맞는 단어를 써 보세요.

1. 이 강아지는 내가 지금까지 본 것 중에서 가장 귀엽다.
   This is the ____________ puppy I've ever seen.
2. 우주비행사들은 달의 암석들을 연구용으로 가져왔다.
   The astronauts brought back ____________ rocks for study.
3. 그의 부모님들은 인근 회사에서 일한다.
   His parents work at a ____________ company.
4. 그녀는 지역 병원에서 자원봉사 활동을 한다.
   She does ____________ work at the local hospital.
5. 그 아이의 손은 꿀을 만져 끈적거린다.
   The child's hands are ____________ with honey.
6. 그녀는 키 크고 날씬한 금발 여성이었다.
   She was a tall ____________ blonde.
7. 어둠침침한 불빛 아래에서 책을 읽으려 하지 말 것.
   Don't try to read under a ____________ light.
8. 무거운 상자들을 너무 많이 들어올려 나는 허리가 아팠다.
   I had a ____________ back from lifting so many heavy boxes.

연습문제 3 영영풀이에 맞는 단어를 써 보세요.

1. ____________ : painful
2. ____________ : covered with something such as gum, etc.
3. ____________ : done of one's own will
4. ____________ : not very bright
5. ____________ : close
6. ____________ : of the moon
7. ____________ : pretty and attractive
8. ____________ : thin, slim

단어 test 21~25일

A 알맞은 단어를 골라서 쓰시오.

public	local	junior	capable	absolute

1. A ____________ beach is for anybody to use.

2. He is two years ____________ to me.

3. Some rulers have ____________ power.

4. It will be 1 a.m. ____________ time when we land.

5. A ____________ mechanic can fix many things.

B 빈칸에 들어갈 알맞은 단어를 고르시오.

1. I always try to be ____________ for appointments.
   a. punctual b. unusual c. different d. normal

2. You are lucky to have such ____________ friends.
   a. disloyal b. constant c. unfaithful d. deceitful

3. It is a ____________ thing to do your best to help the poor.
   a. competent b. skilled c. unqualified d. noble

4. The jury found her ____________ of murder.
   a. guilty b. proper c. important d. honest

5. I am ____________ with the roads here.
   a. common b. familiar c. ordinary d. formal

C 빈칸에 들어갈 단어의 알맞은 형태를 고르시오.

1. She is a ____________ speaker of English.
   a. fluent　　b. fluently　　c. fluence

2. He is ____________ about the results of the examination.
   a. anxiety　　b. anxious　　c. anxiously

3. Most areas of the United States have a ____________ climate.
   a. temperature　　b. temperate　　c. temperament

4. The old friends were ____________ to each other.
   a. loyalty　　b. loyal　　c. loyalist

5. Humans are ____________ beings and must die.
   a. mortal　　b. mortally　　c. mortality

D 다음 주어진 단어를 문맥에 맞게 고치시오.

1. She was (upset)____________ that he hadn't written.

2. He suffered a (minority) ____________ injury on the head.

3. Her family lives in (relate)____________ comfort.

4. These two caps are so (similarity)____________ that it's hard to tell them apart.

5. The bus terminal is in the (center)____________ area of the city.

단어공부 26일째

따라하기 단어를 세 번씩 따라 써보세요.

401 **scholar** [skάlər]	n. 학자
402 **nature** [néitʃər]	n. ❶ 자연 ❷ 성질, 본성
403 **haste** [heist]	n. 서두름
404 **sort** [sɔːrt]	n. 종류(= kind) v. 분류하다
405 **infant** [ínfənt]	n. 유아 a. 유아의, 초기의 ▶ infancy : n. 유아기
406 **army** [άːrmi]	n. ❶ 군대 ❷ 무리, 떼
407 **devil** [dévəl]	n. 악마, 마귀
408 **leisure** [líːʒər]	n. 여가 a. 한가한(= free)

연습문제 1 영어는 우리말로, 우리말은 영어로 써 보세요.

1. devil ______	1. 서두름 ______
2. infant ______	2. 여가 ______
3. nature ______	3. 유아 ______
4. sort ______	4. 학자 ______
5. leisure ______	5. 자연 ______
6. army ______	6. 악마 ______
7. scholar ______	7. 종류 ______
8. haste ______	8. 군대 ______

연습문제 2 문장에 알맞는 단어를 써 보세요.

1. 회관이 육군장교들로 메워졌다.
The hall was filled with ____________ officers.

2. 우리는 버스를 안 놓치려고 급히 서둘러 떠났다.
We left in great ____________ so we wouldn't miss the bus.

3. 꿈 속에서 악마가 그에게 나타났다.
The ____________ appeared to him in a dream.

4. 우리는 자연의 아름다움을 즐기려고 호숫가에 캠프를 쳤다.
We camped beside a lake to enjoy the beauties of ____________.

5. 그 여자는 팔에 아기를 안고 가고 있었다.
The woman was carrying an ____________ in her arms.

6. 그 바쁜 농부는 여가가 별로 없었다.
The busy farmer did not have much ____________.

7. 그는 생물학 분야의 대학자로서 추앙받았다.
He was respected as a great ____________ in the field of biology.

8. 우리는 모든 종류의 과일을 샀다.
We bought all ____________ of fruits.

연습문제 3 영영풀이에 맞는 단어를 써 보세요.

1. ____________ : a kind, a type

2. ____________ : large armed group

3. ____________ : a person of great learning

4. ____________ : the act of hurrying

5. ____________ : an evil being

6. ____________ : all the plants, animals and life on earth

7. ____________ : the time free from work

8. ____________ : baby

단어공부 26일째

따라하기 단어를 세 번씩 따라 써보세요.

409 **merchant** [mə́:rtʃənt]	n. 상인
410 **community** [kəmjú:nəti]	n. 지역사회, 공동체
411 **souvenir** [sù:vəníər]	n. 기념품
412 **parcel** [pɑ́:rsəl]	n. 소포, 소화물(= package)
413 **sorrow** [sɔ́:rou]	n. 슬픔(↔joy)
414 **opinion** [əpínjən]	n. 의견, 견해
415 **shelter** [ʃéltər]	n. ❶ 피난처 ❷ 집(= housing) v. 보호하다, 피난처를 제공하다
416 **cereal** [síəriəl]	n. ❶ 곡물(= grain) ❷ 곡물 가공식품

연습문제 1 영어는 우리말로, 우리말은 영어로 써 보세요.

1. souvenir ________
2. sorrow ________
3. merchant ________
4. shelter ________
5. parcel ________
6. cereal ________
7. community ________
8. opinion ________

1. 지역사회 ________
2. 의견 ________
3. 기념품 ________
4. 곡물 ________
5. 상인 ________
6. 피난처 ________
7. 소포 ________
8. 슬픔 ________

연습문제 2 문장에 알맞는 단어를 써 보세요.

1. 사람들은 자기들이 아끼는 사람이 죽으면 슬픔을 느낀다.
   People feel ____________ when someone they love dies.
2. 폭우가 몰아치는 동안 우리는 동굴로 피신했다.
   During the storm, we took ____________ in a cave.
3. 나는 파리 방문 기념품으로 이 모자를 샀다.
   I bought this hat as a ____________ of my visit to Paris.
4. 나의 조부모님들은 시골 지역에 사신다.
   My grandparents live in a rural ____________.
5. 아침식사로 어떤 곡물식을 드시겠습니까?
   What kind of ____________ would you like for breakfast?
6. 내 의견으로는 그가 경주에서 이길 것이다.
   In my ____________, he will win the race.
7. 베니스는 부유한 상인들의 도시였다.
   Venice was a city of rich ____________.
8. 그녀는 우편으로 부치려고 소포에 주소를 썼다.
   She addressed the ____________ for mailing.

연습문제 3 영영풀이에 맞는 단어를 써 보세요.

1. ____________ : deep sadness
2. ____________ : a place of safety
3. ____________ : a group of people living together in one place or area
4. ____________ : something wrapped in paper
5. ____________ : food made from grain
6. ____________ : a person that buys and sells goods
7. ____________ : what someone thinks about something
8. ____________ : something bought to remember a place

단어공부 27일째

따라하기 단어를 세 번씩 따라 써보세요.

417 **flood** [flʌd]	n. 홍수 v. 범람시키다
418 **thorn** [θɔːrn]	n. (식물의) 가시 ▶ thorny : a. 가시가 있는
419 **drought** [draut]	n. 가뭄
420 **horror** [hɔ́ːrər]	n. 공포, 전율 ▶ horrible : a. 무서운
421 **ash** [æʃ]	n. 재
422 **role** [roul]	n. 역할
423 **sum** [sʌm]	n. ❶ 합계 ❷ 금액
424 **charge** [tʃɑːrdʒ]	n. ❶ 요금 ❷ 담당 v. 청구하다

연습문제 1 영어는 우리말로, 우리말은 영어로 써 보세요.

1. horror ______
2. sum ______
3. thorn ______
4. role ______
5. drought ______
6. flood ______
7. charge ______
8. ash ______

1. (식물의) 가시 ______
2. 역할 ______
3. 재 ______
4. 홍수 ______
5. 요금 ______
6. 공포 ______
7. 합계 ______
8. 가뭄 ______

연습문제 2 | 문장에 알맞는 단어를 써 보세요.

1. 가뭄으로 전국에 기근이 생겼다.
The ____________ caused famine throughout the country.

2. 그녀는 교내 연극에서 주인공 역할을 했다.
She played the leading ____________ in the school play.

3. 홍수는 많은 피해를 줄 수 있다.
____________ can do much damage.

4. 2+3의 합은 5이다.
The ____________ of two and three is five.

5. 그 건물은 타서 재가 되었다.
The building was burned to ____________.

6. 가시 없는 장미는 없다.
There is no rose without a ____________.

7. 우리는 그 꾸러미를 요금을 받지않고 보내드립니다.
We will send the package free of ____________.

8. 나는 거미에 대한 공포가 있다.
I have a ____________ of spiders.

연습문제 3 | 영영풀이에 맞는 단어를 써 보세요.

1. ____________ : a strong fear or dread
2. ____________ : a part played by an actor or actress
3. ____________ : a large amount of water covering dry land
4. ____________ : the total numbers or quantities
5. ____________ : the part left after something burns
6. ____________ : a sharp point on the stem of a plant
7. ____________ : a price, fee, or cost
8. ____________ : a time of little or no rainfall

단어공부 27일째

따라하기 단어를 세 번씩 따라 써보세요.

425 **fee** [fiː]	n. ❶ (전문가의 서비스에 대한) 수수료 ❷ (학교·협회의) 납부금
426 **fare** [fɛər]	n. (배·기차·버스 등의) 요금, 운임
427 **sweat** [swet]	n. 땀 v. 땀을 흘리다
428 **tissue** [tíʃuː]	n. (생물의) 조직
429 **scale** [skeil]	n. ❶ 규모, 크기 ❷ 저울
430 **shape** [ʃeip]	n. 모양, 형상 v. (~모양으로) 만들다
431 **craft** [kræft]	n. ❶ 솜씨, 기술 (= skill) ❷ 공예
432 **slave** [sleiv]	n. 노예 ▶ slavery : n. 노예 신분; 노예 제도

연습문제 1 영어는 우리말로, 우리말은 영어로 써 보세요.

1. sweat ________
2. shape ________
3. fee ________
4. scale ________
5. craft ________
6. tissue ________
7. fare ________
8. slave ________

1. 수수료 ________
2. 노예 ________
3. 모양, 형상 ________
4. (생물의) 조직 ________
5. 규모 ________
6. 요금, 운임 ________
7. 솜씨, 기술 ________
8. 땀 ________

연습문제 2 문장에 알맞는 단어를 써 보세요.

1. 신경조직은 뇌에서 여타 신체 부분에 메시지를 전한다.
   The nervous ____________ sends messages from the brain to other parts of the body.
2. 모든 원은 모양이 똑같다.
   All circles have the same ____________.
3. 땀은 체온을 유지하는 데 도움을 준다.
   ____________ helps to keep the body cool.
4. 목수는 훌륭한 솜씨로 진열장을 만들었다.
   The carpenter made a cabinet with great ____________.
5. 우리 모두는 습관의 노예들이다.
   We are all ____________ of habit.
6. 런던의 버스요금은 꽤 비싸다.
   Bus ____________ in London are quite expensive.
7. 우주의 규모를 상상하기는 어렵다.
   It is hard to imagine the ____________ of the universe.
8. 보험회사는 내 의료비의 일부를 지불했다.
   The insurance company paid some of my medical ____________.

연습문제 3 영영풀이에 맞는 단어를 써 보세요.

1. ____________ : money paid for a service
2. ____________ : an outline or form of something
3. ____________ : the groups of cells forming the parts of animals or plants
4. ____________ : the cost of a ride, such as on a bus, train, or boat
5. ____________ : a skill, especially in making things by hand
6. ____________ : the liquid coming through the skin when it is hot
7. ____________ : a relative size or degree
8. ____________ : a person owned by someone else

단어공부 28일째

따라하기 단어를 세 번씩 따라 써보세요.

433 **item** [áitəm]	n. ❶ 항목, 품목 ❷ (신문 기사의) 한 항목
434 **athlete** [ǽθliːt]	n. 운동선수 ▶ athletic : a. 운동 경기의
435 **strength** [streŋθ]	n. (정신적·신체적) 힘 ▶ strengthen : v. 강화하다
436 **germ** [dʒəːrm]	n. 세균, 병균
437 **dusk** [dʌsk]	n. 어스름, 황혼(↔dawn)
438 **jail** [dʒeil]	n. 감옥(= prison) v. 투옥하다
439 **horizon** [həráizn]	n. 수평선, 지평선 ▶ horizontal : a. 수[지]평선의
440 **shore** [ʃɔːr]	n. (호수·하천의) 물가

연습문제 1 영어는 우리말로, 우리말은 영어로 써 보세요.

1. strength ______
2. jail ______
3. item ______
4. shore ______
5. germ ______
6. horizon ______
7. athlete ______
8. dusk ______

1. 세균, 병균 ______
2. (호수·하천의)물가 ______
3. 운동선수 ______
4. 어스름, 황혼 ______
5. 수평선, 지평선 ______
6. 항목, 품목 ______
7. 감옥 ______
8. (정신적·신체적) 힘 ______

연습문제 2 문장에 알맞는 단어를 써 보세요.

1. 병균을 퍼뜨리지 않게 입을 막고 기침을 하세요.
   Cover your cough so you won't spread ____________.

2. 그 우표 수집첩에는 희귀 종들이 많다.
   There are many rare ____________ in that stamp collection.

3. 우리는 수평선 상의 배 한 척을 보았다.
   We saw a ship on the ____________.

4. 가로등은 땅거미가 질 때 켜진다.
   The street lights go on at ____________.

5. 그 선수는 올림픽에서 금메달을 땄다.
   The ____________ won a gold medal in the Olympics.

6. 우리 물가를 걸어볼까?
   How about walking along the ____________?

7. 그는 체력을 증진하려고 역기를 든다.
   He lifts weights to develop his ____________.

8. 그는 30일간 투옥되었다.
   He was sent to ____________ for 30 days.

연습문제 3 영영풀이에 맞는 단어를 써 보세요.

1. ____________ : a prison
2. ____________ : an object
3. ____________ : the line where the earth and sky seem to meet
4. ____________ : the time of day between sunset and total darkness
5. ____________ : a person who is good at sports
6. ____________ : the sandy or rocky area of land next to the sea
7. ____________ : physical power
8. ____________ : a very small living thing that causes disease

단어공부 28일째

따라하기 단어를 세 번씩 따라 써보세요.

441 **coast** [koust]	n. 해안, 연안 ▶ coastal : a. 연안의
442 **crew** [kruː]	n. 승무원; 선원
443 **score** [skɔːr]	n. 득점, 점수, 성적
444 **skeleton** [skélətn]	n. 골격, 해골
445 **scar** [skɑːr]	n. 흉터 v. 흉터를 남기다
446 **mystery** [místəri]	n. 신비, 불가사의 ▶ mysterious : a. 신비로운
447 **vehicle** [víːhikl]	n. 차량
448 **pride** [praid]	n. ❶ 자부심 ❷ 자만심 ▶ proud : a. 자랑하는, 교만한

연습문제 1 영어는 우리말로, 우리말은 영어로 써 보세요.

1. skeleton ______	1. 흉터 ______
2. crew ______	2. 해안, 연안 ______
3. vehicle ______	3. 차량 ______
4. scar ______	4. 득점, 점수 ______
5. coast ______	5. 자부심 ______
6. pride ______	6. 승무원, 선원 ______
7. score ______	7. 신비, 불가사의 ______
8. mystery ______	8. 골격, 해골 ______

연습문제 2 문장에 알맞는 단어를 써 보세요.

1. 그는 무릎에 흉터가 있다.
He has a ____________ on his knee.

2. 승객과 승무원들 모두 추락사고에서 살아남았다.
All the passengers and ____________ survived the crash.

3. 그의 갑작스러운 죽음은 우리들 모두에게 불가사의한 일로 남아 있다.
His sudden death remains a ____________ to us all.

4. 남해안이 그 나라에서 가장 따뜻한 지역이다.
The south ____________ is the warmest part of the country.

5. 그들은 자식의 성공에 자부심을 가졌다.
They took ____________ in their son's success.

6. 그의 영어시험 점수는 100점이었다.
His ____________ on the English test was 100 percent.

7. 탐험가들은 동굴에서 해골을 발견했다.
The explorers discovered a ____________ in the cave.

8. 공원 안에는 어떤 차량도 진입할 수 없다.
No ____________ are permitted inside the park.

연습문제 3 영영풀이에 맞는 단어를 써 보세요.

1. ____________ : a mark on the skin left after an injury, etc.

2. ____________ : the number of points earned in a contest or test

3. ____________ : something used to carry people or things

4. ____________ : land near the ocean

5. ____________ : the feeling that one is better than other people

6. ____________ : the workers on a ship, airplane, etc.

7. ____________ : something strange or secret

8. ____________ : the bones of an animal or person

단어공부 29일째

따라하기 단어를 세 번씩 따라 써보세요.

449 **channel** [tʃǽnl]	n. ❶ 해협 ❷ 주파수대
450 **harbor** [hɑ́ːrbər]	n. 항구(= port) v. (범인 따위)를 숨기다; (나쁜 마음 따위)를 품다
451 **baggage** [bǽgidʒ]	n. (여행용)짐(= luggage), 수하물
452 **monument** [mɑ́njəmənt]	n. 기념비(탑); 기념물
453 **itch** [itʃ]	n. 가려움; 갈망 v. 가렵다 ▶ itchy : a. 가려운, 갈망하는
454 **benefit** [bénəfit]	n. (물질적·정신적)이익 v. ~에게 도움이 되다, 이롭다
455 **advantage** [ædvǽntidʒ]	n. 이점(↔ disadvantage)
456 **profit** [prɑ́fit]	n. 이익, 수익 ▶ profitable : a. 이익이 많은

연습문제 1 영어는 우리말로, 우리말은 영어로 써 보세요.

1. itch ______
2. channel ______
3. advantage ______
4. baggage ______
5. profit ______
6. harbor ______
7. benefit ______
8. monument ______

1. 가려움, 갈망 ______
2. 항구 ______
3. 이점 ______
4. 해협 ______
5. 기념비, 기념물 ______
6. 이익, 수익 ______
7. (여행용)짐 ______
8. (물질적·정신적)이익 ______

연습문제 2 문장에 알맞는 단어를 써 보세요.

1. 매년 봄이 되면 그는 여행하고 싶어 몸이 근질거린다(여행하고 싶어 못 견딘다).
   Every spring he gets an ____________ to travel.

2. 저 동상은 전몰자 위령비이다.
   That statue is a ____________ to our war dead.

3. 영국해협은 북해와 대서양 사이에 있다.
   The English ____________ lies between the North Sea and the Atlantic Ocean.

4. 세계평화는 인류에 커다란 이익이 될 것이다.
   World peace would be of great ____________ to mankind.

5. 우리는 땅꺼미가 질 때 항구에 도착했다.
   We reached the ____________ at dusk.

6. 당신은 수익을 얼마나 냈습니까?
   How much ____________ did you make?

7. 짐은 몇 개나 됩니까?
   How many pieces of ____________ do you have?

8. 대도시에 살면 많은 이점이 있다.
   Living in a big city has many ____________.

연습문제 3 영영풀이에 맞는 단어를 써 보세요.

1. ____________ : bags, suitcases, etc.
2. ____________ : a good feature; benefit
3. ____________ : a waterway
4. ____________ : a feeling on the skin making someone want to scratch
5. ____________ : money gained in business
6. ____________ : a place where ships can stay safely
7. ____________ : something helpful
8. ____________ : something built in memory of a person or historical event

단어공부 29일째

따라하기 단어를 세 번씩 따라 써보세요.

457 **favor** [féivər]	n. 친절한 행위, 은혜 v. ~에 호의를 보이다, 편들다
458 **fortune** [fɔ́:rtʃən]	n. ❶ 운 ❷ 재산 ▶ fortunate : a. 운 좋은
459 **opportunity** [ὰpərtú:nəti]	n. 기회
460 **misfortune** [misfɔ́:rtʃən]	n. 불운, 불행(= bad luck)
461 **occasion** [əkéiʒən]	n. ❶ (특정한)때 ❷ (특별한)행사 ▶ occasional : a. 이따금의
462 **feature** [fí:tʃər]	n. ❶ 특징 ❷ 얼굴 생김, 이목구비
463 **economy** [ikɑ́nəmi]	n. ❶ 경제 ❷ 절약 ▶ economic : a. 경제의
464 **figure** [fígjər]	n. ❶ 모습 ❷ 숫자

연습문제 1 영어는 우리말로, 우리말은 영어로 써 보세요.

1. occasion ________	1. 기회 ________
2. economy ________	2. 특징 ________
3. misfortune ________	3. 친절한 행위 ________
4. favor ________	4. 경제; 절약 ________
5. figure ________	5. 운; 재산 ________
6. fortune ________	6. 모습 ________
7. feature ________	7. 불운, 불행 ________
8. opportunity ________	8. (특정한)때 ________

연습문제 2 문장에 알맞는 단어를 써 보세요.

1. 불행은 항상 겹쳐 온다.
   ____________ never come to single.

2. 그 사전은 유용한 특징이 많다.
   The dictionary has many useful ____________.

3. 부탁 좀 드려도 되겠습니까?
   Would you do me a ____________?

4. 그녀는 자기 앞의 한 남자의 모습을 보았다.
   She saw the ____________ of a man ahead of her.

5. 그에게는 운이 따르지 않았다.
   ____________ did not favor him.

6. 경제가 불황이다.
   The ____________ is not in good shape.

7. 나는 요즘 여행을 할 기회가 많지 않았다.
   I haven't had much ____________ to travel recently.

8. 나는 그를 몇 차례 만난 적이 있다.
   I have met him on several ____________.

연습문제 3 영영풀이에 맞는 단어를 써 보세요.

1. ____________ : bad luck
2. ____________ : a helpful act; a good turn
3. ____________ : a person's shape
4. ____________ : a time when something happens
5. ____________ : an important part of something
6. ____________ : a chance to do something
7. ____________ : the system by which money, industry and trade are controlled
8. ____________ : chance, (good or bad) luck

단어공부 30일째

따라하기 단어를 세 번씩 따라 써보세요.

465 **commerce** [kámәːrs]	n. 상업, 통상 ▶ commercial : a. 상업의
466 **trade** [treid]	n. 무역, 교역 v. 교환하다
467 **labor** [léibәr]	n. 노동(↔capital)
468 **wage** [weidʒ]	n. (육체노동자의) 임금
469 **income** [ínkʌm]	n. 소득, 수입
470 **author** [ɔ́ːθәr]	n. 저자, 필자
471 **article** [áːrtikl]	n. ❶ 기사 ❷ 물품, 상품
472 **border** [bɔ́ːrdәr]	n. 경계(= boundary)

연습문제 1 영어는 우리말로, 우리말은 영어로 써 보세요.

1. trade ________
2. article ________
3. commerce ________
4. border ________
5. labor ________
6. income ________
7. author ________
8. wage ________

1. 노동 ________
2. 저자, 필자 ________
3. (육체노동자의) 임금 ________
4. 상업 ________
5. 경계 ________
6. 무역, 교역 ________
7. 기사 ________
8. 소득, 수입 ________

연습문제 2 문장에 알맞는 단어를 써 보세요.

1. 사람은 소득 범위 내에서 생활해야 한다.
   You must live within your ____________.
2. 그는 상업에 종사하고 있다.
   He is engaged in ____________.
3. 그들은 발각되지 않고 국경을 넘었다.
   They got across the ____________ without being noticed.
4. 그는 그 공장에서 상당한 액수의 임금을 번다.
   He earns a good ____________ at the factory.
5. 두 나라간의 무역은 금년에 감소했다.
   ____________ between the two countries has decreased this year.
6. 그 과학자는 잡지에 우주여행 기사를 썼다.
   The scientist wrote an ____________ on space travel for the magazine.
7. 그들은 여름을 육체노동을 하며 보냈다.
   They spent the summer doing physical ____________.
8. 그녀는 베스트셀러 소설의 작가이다.
   She is the ____________ of a best-selling novel.

연습문제 3 영영풀이에 맞는 단어를 써 보세요.

1. ____________ : hard work
2. ____________ : someone who writes books, novels, etc.
3. ____________ : the act of buying, selling, or exchanging goods
4. ____________ : the line between nations
5. ____________ : money earned by working, etc.
6. ____________ : the buying and selling on a large scale
7. ____________ : a story written for a newspaper or magazine
8. ____________ : a regular amount of money received for work done

단어공부 30일째

따라하기 | 단어를 세 번씩 따라 써보세요.

473 **address** [ədrés]	n. ❶ 주소 ❷ 연설			
474 **value** [vǽlju:]	n. 가치; 가격 ▶ valuable : a. 귀중한, 고가의			
475 **audience** [ɔ́:diəns]	n. 청중			
476 **dignity** [dígnəti]	n. 존엄, 위엄, 품위			
477 **certificate** [sərtífəkit]	n. 증명서			
478 **antique** [æntí:k]	n. 골동품 a. 옛날의, 예전의			
479 **pottery** [pátəri]	n. 도기(류)			
480 **degree** [digrí:]	n. ❶ 정도(= extent) ❷ (온도의) 도(度)			

연습문제 1 | 영어는 우리말로, 우리말은 영어로 써 보세요.

1. certificate ____________
2. value ____________
3. pottery ____________
4. audience ____________
5. degree ____________
6. address ____________
7. antique ____________
8. dignity ____________

1. 존엄, 위엄 ____________
2. 골동품 ____________
3. 주소; 연설 ____________
4. 정도 ____________
5. 가치; 가격 ____________
6. 도기(류) ____________
7. 청중 ____________
8. 증명서 ____________

연습문제 2 문장에 알맞는 단어를 써 보세요.

1. 나는 귀중한 한국 고대 도기들을 수집해놓고 있다.
   I have a valuable collection of ancient Korean ____________.

2. 그녀는 그러한 모욕에도 품위를 지켰다.
   She kept her ____________ despite the insult.

3. 이 편지에 쓰인 주소를 읽을 수가 없다.
   I can't read the ____________ on this letter.

4. 그 박물관에는 식민지 시대 미국의 골동품들이 있다.
   The museum has ____________ from the time of colonial America.

5. 그 발견은 커다란 가치가 있었다.
   The discovery was of great ____________.

6. 그녀는 어느 정도 믿을 수 있다.
   She can be trusted to some ____________.

7. 그 토론회에는 청중이 많았다.
   There was a large ____________ at the debate.

8. 이 차의 소유 증명서를 보여주세요.
   Please show me your ____________ of ownership for this car.

연습문제 3 영영풀이에 맞는 단어를 써 보세요.

1. ____________ : people gathered to hear a singer, etc. or watch a play, etc.
2. ____________ : things made of soft clay and then baked until hard
3. ____________ : a formal document that states a fact
4. ____________ : extent, amount
5. ____________ : calm and serious behavior
6. ____________ : a place where someone lives and mail is received
7. ____________ : something that is old and valuable
8. ____________ : worth; usefulness

단어 test 25~30일

A 알맞은 단어를 골라서 쓰시오.

sorrow	role	fares	souvenir	leisure

1. The busy farmer did not have much ____________.
2. People feel ____________ when someone they love dies.
3. I bought this hat as a ____________ of my visit to Paris.
4. She played the leading ____________ in the school play.
5. Bus ____________ in London are quite expensive.

B 빈칸에 들어갈 알맞은 단어를 고르시오.

1. The English ____________ lies between the North Sea and the Atlantic Ocean.
   a. sky　　b. earth　　c. Channel　　d. bridge
2. I haven't had much ____________ to travel recently.
   a. moment　　b. case　　c. opportunity　　d. turn
3. You must live within your ____________.
   a. income　　b. spend　　c. profits　　d. yield
4. He earns a good ____________ at the factory.
   a. labor　　b. wage　　c. raise　　d. campaign
5. The scientist wrote an ____________ on space travel for the magazine.
   a. item　　b. thing　　c. piece　　d. article

C 빈칸에 들어갈 단어의 알맞은 형태를 고르시오.

1. She kept her ___________ despite the insult.
   a. dignified b. dignity c. dignitary

2. The discovery was of great ___________.
   a. value b. valuable c. valuate

3. We camped beside a lake to enjoy the beauties of ___________.
   a. natural b. nature c. naturalborn

4. We will send the package free of ___________.
   a. charge b. chargeable c. chargeaholic

5. I have a ___________ of spiders.
   a. horrible b. horribly c. horror

D 다음 주어진 단어를 문맥에 맞게 고치시오.

1. He was respected as a great (scholarly)___________ in the field of biology.

2. Venice was a city of rich (merchandise)___________.

3. We saw a ship on the (horizontal)___________.

4. His sudden death remains a (mysterious)___________ to us all.

5. World peace would be of great (beneficial)___________ to mankind.

특목고 · 내신 대비 어휘 정복 프로젝트!!

Top Vocabulary

Workbook

중급 Level 1

WorldCom ELT

단어퀴즈 1일째

Score /32

학년 반 이름

1	**approach**	9	**pretend**
2	**harm**	10	**imitate**
3	**damage**	11	**affect**
4	**attack**	12	**consider**
5	**choke**	13	**pause**
6	**bite**	14	**amuse**
7	**blow**	15	**dine**
8	**fling**	16	**entertain**

1	불다	9	영향을 미치다
2	공격하다	10	식사하다
3	접근하다	11	모방하다
4	해치다	12	즐겁게 해주다
5	내던지다	13	고려하다
6	손상시키다	14	흥겹게 하다
7	질식시키다	15	~인 체하다
8	물어 뜯다	16	잠시 중지하다

단어퀴즈 2일째

학년 반 이름

Score /32

1 **excite**		9 **fold**	
2 **thrill**		10 **drift**	
3 **amaze**		11 **recite**	
4 **smash**		12 **imagine**	
5 **astonish**		13 **assume**	
6 **impress**		14 **split**	
7 **reap**		15 **commit**	
8 **faint**		16 **doubt**	

1 졸도하다		9 표류하다	
2 깜짝 놀라게 하다		10 상상하다	
3 박살내다		11 의심하다	
4 몹시 놀라게 하다		12 쪼개다	
5 흥분시키다		13 지르다	
6 수확하다		14 가정하다	
7 가슴 설레게 하다		15 접다	
8 깊은 인상을 주다		16 암송하다	

단어퀴즈 3일째

Score /32

학년 반 이름

1 **suspect** ______

2 **shrug** ______

3 **collide** ______

4 **intend** ______

5 **decide** ______

6 **accomplish** ______

7 **shrink** ______

8 **gain** ______

9 **emit** ______

10 **locate** ______

11 **long** ______

12 **achieve** ______

13 **determine** ______

14 **perform** ______

15 **gather** ______

16 **cling** ______

---

1 의도하다 ______

2 ~라고 생각하다 ______

3 줄다 ______

4 충돌하다 ______

5 움츠리다 ______

6 이룩하다 ______

7 얻다 ______

8 결심하다 ______

9 내뿜다 ______

10 갈망하다 ______

11 수행하다 ______

12 (장소를)찾아내다 ______

13 달성하다 ______

14 달라붙다 ______

15 모으다 ______

16 결정하다 ______

단어퀴즈 4일째

Score /32

학년 반 이름 ______

1 **skip** ______

2 **connect** ______

3 **vote** ______

4 **quarrel** ______

5 **misunderstand** ______

6 **judge** ______

7 **educate** ______

8 **acquire** ______

9 **ban** ______

10 **obtain** ______

11 **stick** ______

12 **rub** ______

13 **blush** ______

14 **grind** ______

15 **chop** ______

16 **communicate** ______

---

1 투표하다 ______

2 연결하다 ______

3 오해하다 ______

4 판단하다 ______

5 습득하다 ______

6 교육하다 ______

7 다투다 ______

8 건너뛰다 ______

9 들러붙다 ______

10 금지하다 ______

11 문지르다 ______

12 붉히다 ______

13 갈다 ______

14 연락하다 ______

15 쳐서 자르다 ______

16 획득하다 ______

단어퀴즈 5일째

Score /32

학년 반 이름 ____________________

1 **sting** ____________________
2 **stab** ____________________
3 **wring** ____________________
4 **pat** ____________________
5 **squeeze** ____________________
6 **flip** ____________________
7 **set** ____________________
8 **suit** ____________________
9 **tame** ____________________
10 **stack** ____________________
11 **tie** ____________________
12 **tack** ____________________
13 **crawl** ____________________
14 **drown** ____________________
15 **save** ____________________
16 **wake** ____________________

---

1 비틀어 짜다 ____________________
2 짜내다 ____________________
3 찌르다 ____________________
4 적합하다 ____________________
5 정하다 ____________________
6 (손끝으로)튀기다 ____________________
7 가볍게 두드리다 ____________________
8 (단검으로)찌르다 ____________________
9 고정시키다 ____________________
10 깨우다 ____________________
11 익사하다 ____________________
12 구조하다 ____________________
13 길들이다 ____________________
14 쌓아올리다 ____________________
15 기다 ____________________
16 매다 ____________________

단어퀴즈 6일째

학년 반 이름

Score /32

1 **boil** ____________

2 **leak** ____________

3 **bathe** ____________

4 **mix** ____________

5 **lure** ____________

6 **roast** ____________

7 **stare** ____________

8 **glance** ____________

9 **scan** ____________

10 **cover** ____________

11 **preserve** ____________

12 **reserve** ____________

13 **serve** ____________

14 **digest** ____________

15 **consume** ____________

16 **appreciate** ____________

---

1 섞다 ____________

2 목욕하다 ____________

3 굽다 ____________

4 빤히 쳐다보다 ____________

5 끓이다 ____________

6 흘끗 보다 ____________

7 끌다 ____________

8 새다 ____________

9 보존하다 ____________

10 제공하다 ____________

11 감사하다 ____________

12 소비하다 ____________

13 소화하다 ____________

14 훑어보다 ____________

15 덮다 ____________

16 예약하다 ____________

단어퀴즈 7일째

Score /32

학년 반 이름

1 **congratulate** ______

2 **compete** ______

3 **attend** ______

4 **navigate** ______

5 **thrive** ______

6 **fasten** ______

7 **export** ______

8 **import** ______

9 **conceal** ______

10 **transport** ______

11 **refuse** ______

12 **admit** ______

13 **allow** ______

14 **comfort** ______

15 **forgive** ______

16 **graduate** ______

---

1 축하하다 ______

2 항해하다 ______

3 번성하다 ______

4 단단히 매다 ______

5 수입하다 ______

6 수출하다 ______

7 경쟁하다 ______

8 출석하다 ______

9 시인하다 ______

10 허용하다 ______

11 수송하다 ______

12 졸업하다 ______

13 숨기다 ______

14 위로하다 ______

15 거절하다 ______

16 용서하다 ______

단어퀴즈 8일째

학년 반 이름

Score /32

1 rob ______
2 commute ______
3 stir ______
4 jog ______
5 flee ______
6 hop ______
7 behave ______
8 suck ______
9 neglect ______
10 boast ______
11 delight ______
12 hire ______
13 afford ______
14 relax ______
15 interest ______
16 satisfy ______

---

1 도망치다 ______
2 통근하다 ______
3 빨다 ______
4 강탈하다 ______
5 천천히 달리다 ______
6 행동하다 ______
7 깡총 뛰다 ______
8 휘젓다 ______
9 즐겁게 하다 ______
10 ~할 여유가 있다 ______
11 긴장을 풀다 ______
12 소홀히 하다 ______
13 흥미있게 하다 ______
14 만족시키다 ______
15 고용하다 ______
16 자랑하다 ______

단어퀴즈 9일째

Score /32

학년 반 이름

1 **chuckle** ______
2 **tickle** ______
3 **slip** ______
4 **bound** ______
5 **sow** ______
6 **tear** ______
7 **sew** ______
8 **wear** ______
9 **lick** ______
10 **slide** ______
11 **dress** ______
12 **weave** ______
13 **whirl** ______
14 **steer** ______
15 **sink** ______
16 **rescue** ______

1 경계를 이루다 ______
2 간질이다 ______
3 씨를 뿌리다 ______
4 꿰매다 ______
5 낄낄 웃다 ______
6 착용하다 ______
7 찢다 ______
8 미끄러지다 ______
9 (실·천을) 짜다 ______
10 침몰하다 ______
11 미끄러지다 ______
12 구조하다 ______
13 핥다 ______
14 (옷을) 입다 ______
15 조종하다 ______
16 빙빙 돌다 ______

단어퀴즈 10일째

학년 반 이름 ________________

Score /32

1 **float** ______________

2 **swallow** ______________

3 **flow** ______________

4 **merge** ______________

5 **note** ______________

6 **celebrate** ______________

7 **bump** ______________

8 **shock** ______________

9 **sprout** ______________

10 **frighten** ______________

11 **freeze** ______________

12 **yell** ______________

13 **pray** ______________

14 **spill** ______________

15 **wipe** ______________

16 **soak** ______________

---

1 흐르다 ______________

2 주목하다 ______________

3 부딪치다 ______________

4 (물에) 뜨다 ______________

5 깜짝 놀라게 하다 ______________

6 삼키다 ______________

7 축하하다 ______________

8 합병하다 ______________

9 닦다 ______________

10 고함치다 ______________

11 겁을 먹게 하다 ______________

12 적시다 ______________

13 엎지르다 ______________

14 싹이 돋다 ______________

15 얼다 ______________

16 기원하다 ______________

단어퀴즈 11일째

Score /32

학년 반 이름

1	**cure**	9	**reflect**
2	**rush**	10	**scrub**
3	**shut**	11	**sense**
4	**slam**	12	**melt**
5	**lock**	13	**control**
6	**erupt**	14	**rest**
7	**glow**	15	**sign**
8	**glare**	16	**associate**

1	쾅 닫다	9	녹다
2	눈부시게 빛나다	10	문지르다
3	급히 하다	11	연상하다
4	(화산이)폭발하다	12	반사하다
5	빨갛게 불타다	13	신호하다
6	치료하다	14	통제하다
7	자물쇠를 채우다	15	쉬다
8	닫다	16	느끼다

단어퀴즈 12일째

학년 반 이름

Score /32

1	**attach**	________	9	**stun**	________
2	**consist**	________	10	**create**	________
3	**compose**	________	11	**arrange**	________
4	**comprise**	________	12	**found**	________
5	**appoint**	________	13	**establish**	________
6	**excel**	________	14	**furnish**	________
7	**develop**	________	15	**equip**	________
8	**cultivate**	________	16	**sparkle**	________

1	~을 구성하다	________	9	갖추게 하다	________
2	지정하다	________	10	정돈하다	________
3	붙이다	________	11	번쩍이다	________
4	발달시키다	________	12	제공하다	________
5	능가하다	________	13	세우다	________
6	이루어져 있다	________	14	실신시키다	________
7	갈다; 재배하다	________	15	설립하다	________
8	~을 포함하다	________	16	창조하다	________

단어퀴즈 13일째

학년 반 이름

Score
/32

1 **polish** ______________
2 **spread** ______________
3 **prepare** ______________
4 **contribute** ______________
5 **decorate** ______________
6 **cooperate** ______________
7 **stretch** ______________
8 **extend** ______________
9 **swell** ______________
10 **promote** ______________
11 **compare** ______________
12 **devise** ______________
13 **drag** ______________
14 **resemble** ______________
15 **block** ______________
16 **prevent** ______________

1 장식하다 ______________
2 연장하다 ______________
3 펴다 ______________
4 준비하다 ______________
5 닦다 ______________
6 협력하다 ______________
7 기여하다 ______________
8 퍼뜨리다 ______________
9 비교하다 ______________
10 막다, 방해하다 ______________
11 닮다 ______________
12 부풀다 ______________
13 방지하다 ______________
14 질질 끌다 ______________
15 승진하다 ______________
16 고안하다 ______________

단어퀴즈 14일째

Score /32

학년 반 이름

1 soar	______	9 possess	______
2 shift	______	10 limp	______
3 stray	______	11 murmur	______
4 remove	______	12 owe	______
5 bear	______	13 pant	______
6 arise	______	14 match	______
7 fix	______	15 endure	______
8 improve	______	16 repair	______

1 제거하다	______	9 중얼거리다	______
2 발생하다	______	10 어울리다	______
3 높이 날다	______	11 소유하다	______
4 개선하다	______	12 빚지고 있다	______
5 길을 잃다	______	13 수리(수선)하다	______
6 고치다	______	14 다리를 절다	______
7 이동하다	______	15 견디어내다	______
8 (열매를) 맺다	______	16 헐떡거리다	______

단어퀴즈 | 15일째

Score /32

학년 반 이름

1 **stagger** ______

2 **replace** ______

3 **wrap** ______

4 **recall** ______

5 **remind** ______

6 **whine** ______

7 **occur** ______

8 **mend** ______

9 **punish** ______

10 **subtract** ______

11 **emerge** ______

12 **fade** ______

13 **starve** ______

14 **wander** ______

15 **multiply** ______

16 **refund** ______

---

1 비틀거리다 ______

2 상기하다 ______

3 징징대다 ______

4 대신하다 ______

5 수선하다 ______

6 상기시키다 ______

7 일어나다 ______

8 싸다 ______

9 나타나다 ______

10 벌주다 ______

11 곱하다 ______

12 굶주리다 ______

13 환불하다 ______

14 빼다 ______

15 떠돌다 ______

16 (색깔이) 바래다 ______

단어퀴즈 16일째

학년 반 이름

Score /32

1 **overtake** ____________
2 **recycle** ____________
3 **advertise** ____________
4 **calculate** ____________
5 **beg** ____________
6 **lay** ____________
7 **realize** ____________
8 **check** ____________
9 **pop** ____________
10 **lean** ____________
11 **tend** ____________
12 **appeal** ____________
13 **exhaust** ____________
14 **tread** ____________
15 **spin** ____________
16 **seize** ____________

1 광고하다 ____________
2 두다, 놓다 ____________
3 따라잡다 ____________
4 확인하다 ____________
5 간청하다 ____________
6 깨닫다 ____________
7 재활용하다 ____________
8 계산하다 ____________
9 붙잡다 ____________
10 기진맥진하게 하다 ____________
11 ~하는 경향이 있다 ____________
12 밟다 ____________
13 매력이 있다 ____________
14 기대다 ____________
15 회전하다 ____________
16 펑 하며 터뜨리다 ____________

단어퀴즈 17일째

Score /32

학년 반 이름

1 **snatch** ______________

2 **grip** ______________

3 **flick** ______________

4 **obey** ______________

5 **yield** ______________

6 **spare** ______________

7 **roam** ______________

8 **pursue** ______________

9 **chase** ______________

10 **aim** ______________

11 **arrest** ______________

12 **patrol** ______________

13 **trace** ______________

14 **postpone** ______________

15 **attempt** ______________

16 **roar** ______________

---

1 아끼다 ______________

2 털어버리다 ______________

3 추적하다 ______________

4 잡아 채다 ______________

5 돌아다니다 ______________

6 산출하다 ______________

7 꽉 쥐다 ______________

8 복종하다 ______________

9 ~의 뒤를 밟다 ______________

10 체포하다 ______________

11 시도하다 ______________

12 뒤쫓다 ______________

13 연기하다 ______________

14 (맹수가)포효하다 ______________

15 겨누다 ______________

16 순찰하다 ______________

단어퀴즈 | 18일째

Score /32

학년 반 이름 ____________

1 **growl** ____________

2 **grab** ____________

3 **sniff** ____________

4 **escape** ____________

5 **avoid** ____________

6 **dare** ____________

7 **resist** ____________

8 **stain** ____________

9 **scold** ____________

10 **blame** ____________

11 **accuse** ____________

12 **announce** ____________

13 **protest** ____________

14 **search** ____________

15 **condemn** ____________

16 **seek** ____________

---

1 탈출하다 ____________

2 억제하다 ____________

3 잡아채다 ____________

4 더럽히다 ____________

5 으르렁거리다 ____________

6 감히 ~하다 ____________

7 (코로)들이마시다 ____________

8 피하다 ____________

9 항의하다 ____________

10 탓하다 ____________

11 ~을 찾다 ____________

12 고발하다 ____________

13 비난하다 ____________

14 꾸짖다 ____________

15 탐색하다 ____________

16 발표하다 ____________

단어퀴즈 19일째

학년 반 이름

Score /32

1 **wag** ______

2 **volunteer** ______

3 **stumble** ______

4 **graze** ______

5 **bare** ______

6 **curious** ______

7 **jealous** ______

8 **immediate** ______

9 **primitive** ______

10 **instant** ______

11 **native** ______

12 **domestic** ______

13 **tense** ______

14 **apt** ______

15 **tough** ______

16 **marine** ______

---

1 벌거벗은 ______

2 자원하다 ______

3 풀을 뜯다 ______

4 즉각적인 ______

5 (꼬리를)흔들다 ______

6 알고 싶어하는 ______

7 비틀거리다 ______

8 질투하는 ______

9 모국의 ______

10 ~하기 쉬운 ______

11 원시적인 ______

12 긴장한 ______

13 질긴 ______

14 즉시의 ______

15 바다의 ______

16 국내의 ______

단어퀴즈 | 20일째

Score /32

학년 반 이름 ______________________

1 **individual** ____________

2 **toxic** ____________

3 **loose** ____________

4 **casual** ____________

5 **particular** ____________

6 **normal** ____________

7 **ordinary** ____________

8 **vital** ____________

9 **available** ____________

10 **convenient** ____________

11 **regular** ____________

12 **accurate** ____________

13 **plain** ____________

14 **vague** ____________

15 **mere** ____________

16 **private** ____________

---

1 보통인 ____________

2 느슨한 ____________

3 평범한 ____________

4 개인의 ____________

5 각별한 ____________

6 절대 필요한 ____________

7 유독한, 독성의 ____________

8 평상복의 ____________

9 정확한 ____________

10 막연한 ____________

11 편리한 ____________

12 단순한 ____________

13 규칙적인 ____________

14 개인의 ____________

15 입수할 수 있는 ____________

16 평이한 ____________

단어퀴즈 | 21일째

학년 반 이름

Score /32

1 **public** ____________

2 **ample** ____________

3 **principal** ____________

4 **splendid** ____________

5 **major** ____________

6 **minor** ____________

7 **prime** ____________

8 **bitter** ____________

9 **absolute** ____________

10 **relative** ____________

11 **main** ____________

12 **sour** ____________

13 **pale** ____________

14 **superior** ____________

15 **inferior** ____________

16 **junior** ____________

---

1 (중요성이) 적은 ____________

2 주요한, 으뜸가는 ____________

3 대부분의 ____________

4 충분한 ____________

5 (맛이) 쓴 ____________

6 공공의 ____________

7 (품질이) 최상의 ____________

8 호화로운 ____________

9 (맛이) 신 ____________

10 우월한 ____________

11 절대적인 ____________

12 손아래의 ____________

13 주된 ____________

14 상대적인 ____________

15 열등한 ____________

16 창백한 ____________

Score /32

학년 반 이름

1 **senior** ______
2 **primary** ______
3 **due** ______
4 **local** ______
5 **sole** ______
6 **universal** ______
7 **brisk** ______
8 **similar** ______
9 **capable** ______
10 **bold** ______
11 **central** ______
12 **grand** ______
13 **bald** ______
14 **enjoyable** ______
15 **billion** ______
16 **punctual** ______

---

1 전세계의 ______
2 (특정) 지역의 ______
3 비슷한 ______
4 주요한; 최초의 ______
5 활발한 ______
6 손위의 ______
7 유일한 ______
8 ~할 예정인 ______
9 시간을 엄수하는 ______
10 중심에 있는 ______
11 유쾌한 ______
12 유능한 ______
13 대머리의 ______
14 십억의 ______
15 대담한 ______
16 웅대한 ______

단어퀴즈 23일째

Score /32

학년 반 이름

1 **sound** ____________

2 **rare** ____________

3 **precious** ____________

4 **pure** ____________

5 **critical** ____________

6 **cunning** ____________

7 **constant** ____________

8 **ideal** ____________

9 **naughty** ____________

10 **noble** ____________

11 **fair** ____________

12 **evil** ____________

13 **pious** ____________

14 **firm** ____________

15 **strict** ____________

16 **ashamed** ____________

---

1 교활한 ____________

2 매우 드문 ____________

3 이상적인 ____________

4 귀중한 ____________

5 변함없는 ____________

6 순수한 ____________

7 건전한 ____________

8 위급한 ____________

9 공평한 ____________

10 부끄러워하는 ____________

11 경건한 ____________

12 숭고한 ____________

13 엄격한 ____________

14 장난꾸러기인 ____________

15 굳은 ____________

16 사악한 ____________

단어퀴즈 | 24일째

Score /32

학년 반 이름

1 **familiar** ____________

2 **shameful** ____________

3 **severe** ____________

4 **upset** ____________

5 **keen** ____________

6 **innocent** ____________

7 **guilty** ____________

8 **handy** ____________

9 **calm** ____________

10 **shy** ____________

11 **anxious** ____________

12 **alike** ____________

13 **extra** ____________

14 **fluent** ____________

15 **excess** ____________

16 **lame** ____________

---

1 가혹한 ____________

2 무죄의 ____________

3 잘 아는 ____________

4 곁에 있는 ____________

5 열심인 ____________

6 부끄러운 ____________

7 유죄의 ____________

8 언짢은 ____________

9 초과하는 ____________

10 걱정하는 ____________

11 유창한 ____________

12 절름발이의 ____________

13 서로 닮은 ____________

14 평온한 ____________

15 여분의 ____________

16 수줍어하는 ____________

단어퀴즈 **25일째**

학년 반 이름

Score /32

1 **greedy** ______________

2 **loyal** ______________

3 **royal** ______________

4 **tropical** ______________

5 **temperate** ______________

6 **mortal** ______________

7 **shallow** ______________

8 **solar** ______________

9 **lunar** ______________

10 **sticky** ______________

11 **dim** ______________

12 **cute** ______________

13 **sore** ______________

14 **slender** ______________

15 **nearby** ______________

16 **voluntary** ______________

1 충성스러운 ______________

2 죽을 운명의 ______________

3 열대 지방의 ______________

4 태양의 ______________

5 온화한 ______________

6 탐욕스러운 ______________

7 얕은 ______________

8 왕의 ______________

9 날씬한 ______________

10 어둠침침한 ______________

11 바로 가까이의 ______________

12 작고 예쁜 ______________

13 달의 ______________

14 자발적인 ______________

15 끈적거리는 ______________

16 아픈 ______________

Score /32

학년 반 이름 ______________________

1 **scholar** ______________________

2 **nature** ______________________

3 **haste** ______________________

4 **sort** ______________________

5 **infant** ______________________

6 **army** ______________________

7 **devil** ______________________

8 **leisure** ______________________

9 **merchant** ______________________

10 **community** ______________________

11 **souvenir** ______________________

12 **parcel** ______________________

13 **sorrow** ______________________

14 **opinion** ______________________

15 **shelter** ______________________

16 **cereal** ______________________

---

1 서두름 ______________________

2 여가 ______________________

3 유아 ______________________

4 학자 ______________________

5 자연 ______________________

6 악마 ______________________

7 종류 ______________________

8 군대 ______________________

9 지역사회 ______________________

10 의견 ______________________

11 기념품 ______________________

12 곡물 ______________________

13 상인 ______________________

14 피난처 ______________________

15 소포 ______________________

16 슬픔 ______________________

단어퀴즈 27일째

Score /32

학년 반 이름

1 **flood**	____	9 **fee**	____
2 **thorn**	____	10 **fare**	____
3 **drought**	____	11 **sweat**	____
4 **horror**	____	12 **tissue**	____
5 **ash**	____	13 **scale**	____
6 **role**	____	14 **shape**	____
7 **sum**	____	15 **craft**	____
8 **charge**	____	16 **slave**	____

---

1 (식물의) 가시	____	9 수수료	____
2 역할	____	10 노예	____
3 재	____	11 모양, 형상	____
4 홍수	____	12 (생물의) 조직	____
5 요금	____	13 규모	____
6 공포	____	14 요금, 운임	____
7 합계	____	15 솜씨, 기술	____
8 가뭄	____	16 땀	____

단어퀴즈 28일째

학년 반 이름

Score /32

1 **item** ______________

2 **athlete** ______________

3 **strength** ______________

4 **germ** ______________

5 **dusk** ______________

6 **jail** ______________

7 **horizon** ______________

8 **shore** ______________

9 **coast** ______________

10 **crew** ______________

11 **score** ______________

12 **skeleton** ______________

13 **scar** ______________

14 **mystery** ______________

15 **vehicle** ______________

16 **pride** ______________

---

1 세균, 병균 ______________

2 (호수·하천의)물가 ______________

3 운동선수 ______________

4 어스름, 황혼 ______________

5 수평선, 지평선 ______________

6 항목, 품목 ______________

7 감옥 ______________

8 (정신적·신체적) 힘 ______________

9 흉터 ______________

10 해안, 연안 ______________

11 차량 ______________

12 득점, 점수 ______________

13 자부심 ______________

14 승무원, 선원 ______________

15 신비, 불가사의 ______________

16 골격, 해골 ______________

단어퀴즈 29일째

학년 반 이름

Score /32

1 **channel** ____________
2 **harbor** ____________
3 **baggage** ____________
4 **monument** ____________
5 **itch** ____________
6 **benefit** ____________
7 **advantage** ____________
8 **profit** ____________
9 **favor** ____________
10 **fortune** ____________
11 **opportunity** ____________
12 **misfortune** ____________
13 **occasion** ____________
14 **feature** ____________
15 **economy** ____________
16 **figure** ____________

1 가려움, 갈망 ____________
2 항구 ____________
3 이점 ____________
4 해협 ____________
5 기념비, 기념물 ____________
6 이익, 수익 ____________
7 (여행용)짐 ____________
8 (물질적·정신적)이익 ____________
9 기회 ____________
10 특징 ____________
11 친절한 행위 ____________
12 경제; 절약 ____________
13 운; 재산 ____________
14 모습 ____________
15 불운, 불행 ____________
16 (특정한)때 ____________

단어퀴즈 30일째

Score /32

학년 반 이름

1 **commerce** ________

2 **trade** ________

3 **labor** ________

4 **wage** ________

5 **income** ________

6 **author** ________

7 **article** ________

8 **border** ________

9 **address** ________

10 **value** ________

11 **audience** ________

12 **dignity** ________

13 **certificate** ________

14 **antique** ________

15 **pottery** ________

16 **degree** ________

---

1 노동 ________

2 저자, 필자 ________

3 (육체노동자의) 임금 ________

4 상업 ________

5 경계 ________

6 무역, 교역 ________

7 기사 ________

8 소득, 수입 ________

9 존엄, 위엄 ________

10 골동품 ________

11 주소; 연설 ________

12 정도 ________

13 가치; 가격 ________

14 도기(류) ________

15 청중 ________

16 증명서 ________

특목고 · 내신 대비 어휘 정복 프로젝트!!

Top Vocabulary

중급 Level 1

Workbook